SECRET NATURE OF BRITAIN

SECRET NATURE OF BRITAIN

ANDREW COOPER

BBC BOOKS

To:

JEANNE,
JULIA &
CHARLES

Published by BBC Books,
a division of BBC Enterprises Limited,
Woodlands, 80 Wood Lane, London W12 0TT
First published 1989

ISBN 0 563 20594 6

Set in 11 on 14pt Kennerley by Ace Filmsetting Ltd, Frome, Somerset
Printed and bound in Great Britain by Richard Clay Ltd, Bungay, Suffolk
Colour separations by Technik Ltd, Berkhamsted
Jacket printed by Belmont Press, Northampton

CONTENTS

ACKNOWLEDGEMENTS

Over the last three years, during the making of the television series and writing of this book, I have met and been helped by many people who have generously shared their knowledge and spared their time. I am most grateful to them all. I owe a great debt of thanks to my colleagues in BBC Television for their support, ideas and skills: to David Spires, the executive producer, and editors Rod Thomas and Justin Smith; to Jenny Slater for production assistance and to George Davies for so much help; and, last but not least, to Phil Speight and everyone at BBC Plymouth for their continued support, humour and professionalism. In London I must thank Elizabeth Parker for the music, John Hale for mixing the sound track and Sebastian Gowar-Cliffe for the title design. For making the series possible I would also like to thank BBC Enterprises, especially John Kelly, Sheila Hamilton and Jackie Whittaker to name but a few.

Wildlife films make many special demands and so special thanks are due to those whose assistance made many of the photographs possible: Roger Hosking, whose own superb work appears in this book, and John Bowers, Brian Knox, Noel Allan, Geoff Kaczanow, Robin Khan, Peter White, Nick Williams and Heather Woodland. I am particularly grateful to all the landowners and managers who allowed me such free access to their grounds – especially Peter Barnes, Lord Courtenay, David Curry, Ellis and Lyn Daw, Mike Henderson, Jeff Norris, Mike Scott and Maurice Williams. Without the help and co-operation I received from so many people, much of my work would not be possible and so I must thank the MoD conservation officer, Colonel James Baker, and the officers and personnel of the armed services at Okehampton and Lulworth Ranges and HMS *Cambridge*. Thanks are also due to the Forestry Commission at Haldon and the clay mining companies of the Bovey Basin.

No amount of personal experience can reveal all the intricate details of animal and plant life and many people have spent a lifetime unravelling some of the extraordinary facts. Their discoveries and descriptions of the way that nature works are the basis on which my wildlife programmes are made. The results of their scientific work are available in specialist journals and books, but on some occasions I have been fortunate enough to have been helped by them personally in the field. I am particularly grateful to Dr David Stradling, Dr Bob Stebbings and Dr Andy Stephens.

For once again finding so many references and books, my thanks are due to the librarian and staff of Newton Abbot Library. Finally, I would like to thank BBC Books for turning my writing into a book, adding accuracy and understanding and a gifted design. I owe a special debt to Susan Kennedy for getting me started. Sheila Ableman, Judy Maxwell, Rachel Hardman and particularly Sarah Hoggett. I thank you all.

INTRODUCTION

There is another world outside people's daily lives, a world where danger and death are everyday events and survival is only of the fittest. But you do not have to travel far to watch nocturnal predators returning with a kill, or to wade through the shallows of a swamp looking for snakes and giant spawning fish, for this is the secret side of Britain – its nature. The British Isles support a greater diversity of wildlife and habitats than almost any other country of similar size in the world. But if you think that all there is to know about the wildlife of Britain has already been discovered, think again. The day-to-day lives of some of the most common species of wildlife remain virtually unknown, and there are still corners of the countryside that remain untrodden by people. The haunting call of the tawny owl and its stunning face are so familiar, yet it is one of the least studied birds in Britain. And it is certainly not alone.

Britain has come a long way since its new beginnings after the last ice age. Over the last three thousand years, since the start of farming, the countryside has seen tremendous change. At no time has that change been so fast, and the influence of people so intense, as today. It sometimes seems as if Britain's native flora and fauna have been banished to just a few unspoilt corners – yet if you know how to look for it, an incredible variety of wildlife can be found amidst the hustle and bustle of human activity.

Secret Nature of Britain sets out to explore the animals and plants that live in places shaped or exploited by man. While the natural succession in a broad-leafed wood sees old trees fall and new growth filling the gaps over hundreds of years, a conifer plantation is a forest with a limited lifespan. Here today, an entire wood could be felled and gone tomorrow. Modern forestry is still maturing and it is only now in the process of harvesting its first crop. As attitudes change, so too will the nature of future forests. Following the fortunes of one particular forest, through wind and fire and the lives of some of its most elusive creatures, reveals that there is far more to a wood than its trees.

A major mining operation which cuts deep into the heart of the countryside has enriched the nation, both financially and in terms of its wildlife. Abandoned pits and subsequent subsidence have flooded to form an amazing series of lakes and a wetland of unique natural interest. In winter only wildfowl are evident, yet throughout the spring and summer the freshwater pools bloom with life.

The building of the railways across Britain also dramatically altered the landscape. Today steam trains, a lingering legacy of bygone days, still ferry tourists along a line renowned for its beauty, rattling past the wildlife that lives alongside the tracks.

The guttural call of ravens, birds whose presence has long been held to symbolise the continuation of the monarchy, echoes around regularly blasted rock-strewn quarries. But as time passes, a returning tide of natural growth softens the sharp edges and ruined surrounds. Some of our rarest mammals now survive in hidden worlds originally found by the quarrymen.

Huge areas of the country are set aside for the training of troops and trial battlegrounds. From open moorland to islands in the sight of guns, these Ministry of Defence lands contain many rare and endangered species. Perhaps the most remarkable site is in a valley near the Dorset coast. A once-thriving village, requisitioned by the army during the Second World War, now lies in ruins; but far from being completely abandoned, the area teems with wildlife – perhaps a last vestige of how much of England looked in medieval times.

The history of Britain and its landowners is closely linked with the hunting of game. While some birds and mammals have led a charmed life protected by punitive laws, many natural predators have been nearly wiped out in the name of game protection. But in contrast to the stripped and clean lines of surrounding farmland, many large estates have retained woodland cover and preserved their hedgerows. Today such estates are among the largest privately owned nature reserves in the country where game birds and mammals continue to thrive.

This book, and the BBC television series which it accompanies, are the result of some three years' research and work in the field. Perhaps not surprisingly, certain scenes stand out in my memory. I shall never forget filming a venomous adder, poised to strike, from a distance of only a few inches. I scrambled across the rocks of a seabird colony, knowing full well that huge guns – loaded with live ammunition – could be trained on the island as a 'safe bearing'. And then there was the day I set out to mimic a fallow deer buck by fixing a pair of cast-off antlers to the camera – and felt the force as a full-grown buck took up the challenge and charged towards me . . . Inevitably, only a small proportion of what I saw could be captured on film, and then there are those that simply got away – but that is another story.

CHAPTER 1

THE EPHEMERAL FOREST

A rising winter sun sent streaks of light between the Douglas firs, which towered around a clearing created by recent felling. Overnight the temperature had dropped to 12 degrees Centigrade below freezing, and a glinting layer of frost cloaked the land. The cold had penetrated deep into the soft needle-strewn soil, making the ground beneath my feet as hard as iron. Only the distant drone of traffic drifting now and then broke for me the spell of total isolation. It was as if all life had been frozen by the intense cold.

Suddenly, the scream of a chainsaw echoed through the forest. A pheasant took noisily to the air and the bobbing white rump of a startled deer disappeared between the trees. The rasping whine of the saw changed tone as its teeth bit into the wood, spewing chippings gouged from the trunk. Leaving the engine to idle, the foresters finally toppled the tree using a hammer and wedge. With a groan of splintering wood, the tree slowly started to move, gathering speed as it crashed towards the ground. Almost before it had settled the men had begun to clear its main trunk of side shoots. Then chains were fastened round one end of its stripped girth and it was hauled onto a nearby transporter. Engines roared, branches crashed and the earth shuddered as more trees were felled.

The idea of planting a future timber crop is far older than this plantation, and the practice of coppicing is thousands of years older than the origin of its name, from the Norman-French word meaning 'to cut'. This was shown in 1973 when a remarkable relic, which had escaped the usual rot and decay, came to light in the wetlands of the Somerset levels. Preserved in the acidity of peat were even-sized poles of oak, ash, alder, lime, hazel and holly, laid across vast stretches of bog. The poles in this 6000-year-old causeway bore all the marks of coppiced growth.

Incredibly, a craft that began in neolithic times survived with little change across the millennia. Many overgrown and neglected woodlands lying scattered across Britain are remnants of a once-thriving rural industry. In medieval times, coppices of ash and hazel were a renewable resource, their small straight trunks cut back to their bases every seven or more years. They were the natural source for tool handles, hurdles and fences, and faggots for the fire. On a different scale, larger slow-growing oak and elm were planted for the benefit of some future generation of craftspeople who would use them to fashion timber-framed houses and furniture, and fleets of wooden ships.

But if the techniques of coppicing have remained much the same, the timber crop has changed markedly over the centuries. The first trees to appear were the great group of cone-bearing trees, which evolved 300 million years ago, long before the broad-leafed trees and other flowering plants. Occurring worldwide, the conifers form the greatest forest on earth, which extends right around the cold north of the globe – a broad band, nearly 2000 kilometres wide in places, crossing North America and spanning Siberia to Scandinavia, thriving wherever there is suitable land.

The conifers include about 100 species of pine. Fast-growing, yet tolerant of a short growing season and long cold winters, the pine survives even at the edge of the Arctic tundra. During winter there, it is continually dark and the temperature can drop to 40 degrees Centigrade below zero. Deep snow covers ground and forest alike and, until the spring thaw, there is no source of free-flowing water. The pine not only endures the weight of laden snow on its branches but also survives a drought as severe as that in any sun-scorched desert.

The tall, tapering shape of the pine helps to prevent it breaking under the weight of snow. When heavily laden, the branches droop down and shed some of their load. Even more important is the design of the leaf which, in common with many other conifers, is needle-like. The long, slender pine needle easily sheds snow, and contains little liquid to freeze. Protected by a thick waxy coat, its dark green colour allows it to absorb maximum warmth from the feeble sunlight. Like all leaves, the pine needle has tiny pores called stomata and some water is necessarily lost to the air through these. However, the pine needle has a smaller surface area and, therefore, far fewer stomata than broad leaves. In addition, the pine's stomata are set in a groove which can be closed when the need arises.

When the last ice age waned, some 10 000 years ago, Britain was still joined to the continental mainland. As the ice sheets shrank, the tree line fringing the Arctic tundra slowly spread northwards. Wind-blown seeds of birch were soon followed by aspen and rowan and then the pine. These pioneering species were adapted to surviving the coldest conditions, and gradually turned the open wilderness into a land shaded and sheltered by a canopy of leaves. As the world's climate warmed, the pine advanced further north, and the broad-leafed hazel, elm, oak and then alder spread up from the south. In place of the needle carpet, a mulch of softer leaves fell each autumn, increasing the fertility of the soil and allowing a variety of other plant life to flourish.

By the time Britain had become an island, some 7000 years ago, lime trees had colonised the south of England. The woodland plants and animals, cut off by the rising seas, were the predecessors of the native wildlife that survives today.

The number and variety of species supported by deciduous woodland is enormous. During the roughly 250-year lifespan of an oak, it may be inhabited by more than 200 different forms of life. Fungi consume the leaves, weevils eat the seedlings, while moth and butterfly caterpillars feast on the summer growth of fresh leaves. Birds, such as warblers and tits, along with some bats, forage for these insects and nest or roost among the branches or inside the trunk. The tree may also support other plants, such as ivy and honeysuckle climbing from the ground, and mosses, ferns and lichens flourishing high above the woodland floor. Squirrels and jays pull off acorns in the autumn while down below mice and voles eat the fallen fruit. These small rodents are food for the tawny owl and the fox. Even the rotting leaf litter supports a life as rich and varied as the tree.

In the north of the country, part of the coniferous forest which had covered Britain during the first millennium after the last ice age still survived. Compared with the rich diversity of life in a deciduous wood, there was little flora and fauna to be found in this vast pine forest; yet the forest was not as dense and gloomy as modern conifer plantations. The birch and the graceful rowan tree flourished in clearings, and sometimes holly or hazel grew alongside the hardy juniper. However, where the majestic pine dominated, excluding light and covering the floor with a stifling mat of needles, few other plants could survive. Among those that did were heather, wintergreens, the fruit-bearing bilberries, cloudberries and crowberries, and even some orchids, such as the lesser twayblade and the coral root. Creeping lady's tresses raised their white-flowered spikes, while among the

Conifers are adapted to survive in harsh, cold conditions, and snow slides easily from the needle-like leaves and drooping branches. Most are evergreen, but the larch (*bottom*) is one of the few conifers that is deciduous.

most attractive plants was the shade-loving, delicate pink twinflower. Most of these plants and many of the animals can be seen today below the Cairngorms, at Beinn Eighe and in Glen Affric, Glen Strathfarrar and the Black Wood of Rannoch. These are the last vestiges of the primeval pine forest that once covered a vast area of Scotland. The larger predators, including the lynx, bear and wolf, have gone, of course, and the remaining wildlife maintains a tenuous hold in the dwindling reserves of native pine woods.

In less than 3000 years, Britain changed from a tree-covered country to a more pastoral land. The forests, both deciduous and coniferous, were gradually reduced by cutting and burning for grazing, and cultivating crops. As populations grew and settled into villages and towns, the human need for timber increased. Trees of 100-year growth were felled to build houses. Fleets warring in the Channel required ships built of the finest hardwood. (A man-o'-war in Nelson's navy, for example, required the felling of 3000 oaks.) Agricultural improvements resulted in the destruction of large tracts of woodland, and the encroachment of industry swallowed up more forest. By the turn of this century, only 5 per cent of Britain was woodland. With the woods had gone the insects, birds and mammals that relied on trees to survive.

A shortage of workable timber during the First World War led to the formation of the Forestry Commission in 1919. Broad-leafed trees, even when coppiced, take a considerable time to grow into substantial trunks, and yield a timber called hardwood. So, with the increasing need for timber, people's attention turned to the faster-growing conifers, which produce a timber better suited to modern needs. (Although called softwood, the timber of conifers is not necessarily softer than that of broad-leafed trees.) Within months the first plantation had been laid out at Eggesford in Devon, and within years thousands of hectares from the south coast of England to Scotland had been turned over to conifers. Of these, only the yew, juniper and Scots pine were native to this country. Douglas firs, Sitka spruce, Lodgepole and Corsican pine marched in regimented rows across the country. Elsewhere, deciduous coppices were cleared to plant larch.

These fast-growing trees were imported from northern Europe and northwest America, and native British species found it difficult or impossible to adapt to life there. The way in which plantations are designed and managed can increase the problems. The close planting of trees results in too much shade for the vast majority of ground-dwelling plants, and few are able to survive among the thick carpet of needles. Trees planted in uniform rows offer little or no variety of habitat for wildlife. Mature trees are cropped as soon as possible, leaving little fallen timber to rot and provide food for fungi and insects, and homes for birds and mammals. Unlike the seasonal shower of broad leaves and the wealth of litter-dwelling life in a deciduous wood, a pine forest is comparatively bare. Conifers do shed their leaves eventually, though not all at the same time. The durability of pine needles largely determines the life that surrounds them. Bacteria and fungi break down the tough needles so slowly that the needles pile up, layer upon layer, stifling other plants. Beneath this carpet, fungal filaments invade every part of the poor, acidic soil, helping to release nutrients. The shallow-rooted pine trees benefit by absorbing the chemicals released. The relationship goes further, for the fungi are also thought to extract some of the food they need directly from the pine's roots. More than 100 different species of fungi have been found associated with just one species of pine, and up to seven have been found living on the roots of a single tree.

The waxy resinous leaves are inedible to all but a few insects and birds. The only British bird able to cope with such a diet is the capercaillie, a large relative of the grouse, which inhabits the far north of the country – and even this bird prefers the more tender spring shoots. Cone seeds attract and sustain a far higher number of mammals and birds. These are the remnant population of a wild community that once covered the whole of Western Europe wherever conifers grew.

Haldon's plantation is a good example of this. The forest was laid out on the slopes of a south Devon hill some seventy years ago, and was only the second created by the then newly formed Forestry Commission. Scots pine planted on the gravel top was the first to take root, while Douglas fir grew on the better soil lower down the slopes. Since then a whole host of pines and foreign firs have steadily increased the forest's size to its present fourteen square kilometres. As exploring Haldon's plantation from within revealed disappointingly little animal life, I climbed to a vantage point high on a hillside. From here the view proved far more rewarding. The sun warmed the forest in the valley below as a mild winter wind gently swayed the tree tops. A series of loud short calls rang out, and an excited flock of crossbills winged their way in purposeful, undulating flight towards a group of pine trees. These are rotund, almost parrot-like birds, the cocks crimson and the hens a more subtle green. They are very gregarious and form social flocks in winter as they feed upon cones. The crossbill extracts the seeds from the cone remarkably swiftly using its curiously crossed beak. Usually, the bird feeds from a cone attached to the branch, but sometimes it will pick the cone off and hold it, parrot-fashion.

The hardest time of the year for crossbills is late summer, when the conifer crop may start to dwindle and the birds may leave their original sites to find new feeding grounds. At first they venture only a short distance. If cones are generally

The great spotted woodpecker (*opposite*) normally collects insects to feed its young but in winter turns its attention to pine cones. The grey squirrel (*below left*) uses its powerful teeth to strip away the scales of the cone, leaving debris scattered on the forest floor (*below right*). The nocturnal woodmouse (*bottom*) is almost as small as the pine cone on which it feeds.

in short supply, they occasionally migrate across Europe, and this may result in a crossbill invasion of the central highlands of Scotland, south and east England, and the moors of Devon.

The extraordinary skew of the beak which gives these birds their name is also the feature that distinguishes the populations in different areas. Those which subsist mainly on Scots pine have larger, deeper beaks than those which live in the continental spruce forest belt, extending from Europe right across Asia. In the far north of Britain a distinct form, known as the Scottish crossbill, survives around the last fragments of the once great Caledonian forest.

While for most birds winter is the most taxing time of year, for crossbills it is a time of plenty. Conifer cones take nearly two years to grow, reaching maturity by the end of the second autumn. They retain their seeds throughout the winter months, and release them in the warm dry days of spring. To take advantage of this, crossbills nest and rear their broods before the annual shedding of seeds. On this cold January morning, a cock bird's scarlet plumage stood out vividly as he sang from the topmost branches of a pine. He had courted a mate by chasing her and then, often, feeding her. Their nest, lodged in the fork of a branch, was a tight collection of twigs, grass, lichen, moss and wool, lined with an inner cup of softer material – finer grass, hair, fur, feathers. The hen did most of the actual building, although the male tagged along sometimes as she fetched nesting material. Now, having laid her eggs, she would sit on the nest hour after hour for nearly two weeks, enduring driving rain and snow, nightly frosts and the dangers of scavenging squirrels. The male plays no part in incubating the eggs or brooding the young. His contribution is to find enough food for himself and his mate until the chicks hatch. Then the hen leaves the nest to join in the search for cones. They feed their growing family exclusively on conifer seeds, unlike many other seed-eating birds, which supplement their young's diet with protein-rich insects.

As the day wore on, I made my way back into the forest to where the crossbills had been feeding. Whenever these birds feed, they produce a steady shower of drifting seed wings and cones with split scales. The partially eaten cones fall onto a spring mat of fallen needles, where the few remaining seeds are seldom wasted. As the sun began to set, a faint rustle gave away the passage of a foraging woodmouse. With large bead-like eyes and rounded ears, this rodent has a sleek, sandy coat fading almost to yellow on the flanks. Its pale underside gleamed as it stood upright on long hind legs, before cautiously approaching a fallen cone, as tall and round as itself. Before feeding, the mouse dragged its find to a sheltered place, away from any keen-eyed predator. Beginning at the base of the cone, it worked its way up and around, manipulating the heavy structure with dexterous front paws. The sharp teeth can gnaw away the scales of even tightly closed cones to reach the seed inside. After a few minutes all that remained was a neatly stripped core, with a tuft of small scales left on top and the rest strewn around.

A shower of rain before dawn and an icy wind left the cones on the pines encased in a layer of ice. It would be some time before the meagre warmth of daylight melted the frozen coat to allow a crossbill to feed. However, the ice is no impediment to the largest and most widespread arboreal rodent in Britain, the grey squirrel. This alien was introduced from North America at the turn of this century, and is now firmly established throughout the country. As in its native land, it lives mainly among hardwoods, but will invade coniferous plantations which lie near broad-leafed woods. The grey squirrel is messier than the mouse and its feeding remains are more straggly, with the base stripped to a point by the squirrel's powerful teeth. The mouse cannot strip the basal scales off and has to gnaw them, leaving a more rounded shape.

If a cone of ripe seeds cannot be torn from a branch, both mice and squirrels will eat it where it grows, stripping all the scales from the side they can reach. Another creature must remove the cone before it can extract the seed. I watched a great spotted woodpecker hack a cone free and fly off with it to an oak tree with a ridged bark. There, the bird wedged the cone firmly into a deep crevice in the trunk. Each scale was twisted off by the chisel-shaped beak, and the long sticky tongue extracted the seed. When one side had been stripped, the bird turned the cone round carefully, always keeping the pointed end uppermost. Even though its bill is powerful enough to hammer through solid wood, it may take a woodpecker up to four minutes and more than 800 blows to finish a single cone. If there are no suitable trees close by, the woodpecker drills a small hole in a trunk to hold the cone still, or secures it in a cavity in a rotten tree base. The tell-tale stripped cones scattered all around show where a stump has been used as a woodpecker's workshop.

The striking black and white plumage of the adult great spotted woodpecker and the vivid crossbill flocks were not the only splashes of winter colour in the conifer plantation. Bright yellow-green siskins are resident all year in increasing numbers wherever there are extensive forests of pine. Once confined only to Scotland and the north of England, they are now widely established from East Anglia to south Devon. Since the early 1960s, British siskins have become regular visitors to many bird tables, flocking in to feed on peanuts. This exploitation of a new food source may explain the expanding range of these attractive birds. The male, which has a distinctive black cap and is brighter yellow than the female, performs a display flight over the nesting territory in spring. In winter,

The fresh coloured pupa of the pine hawk moth (*below*) is revealed after the old caterpillar skin is shed in early autumn. In a few hours it will turn brown, matching the forest floor on which it lies. Its caterpillar (*bottom*) is one of the few insects able to feed on conifer leaves. The adult moth (*opposite*) emerges in summer.

siskins flock in large twittering groups among the branches, along with another sociable seed-eating bird, the lesser redpoll. As well as frequenting conifers, alder and birch, the redpoll can also be found with other finches on farmland.

Towards the end of winter, warm March days hinted that spring had come. But Britain's weather is anything but predictable. The wind began to strengthen from the west, and dark heavy clouds came racing in across Dartmoor towards Haldon's forested hill, heralding the tail end of a hurricane that had swept across the Atlantic. The storm raged all night and dawn broke to floods of rain and a howling wind. As I picked my way back into the forest, the clouds cleared for a few moments, and the sun lit up a transformed scene. Whole trees had been torn from the ground as if by a giant hand, their uplifted root boles leaving craters in the ground. Others had been snapped in two like matchwood. The roar of the wind was deafening as a great gust brought down more trees in quick succession – each one with an agonising groan and tearing of roots. Cones and branches of all sizes were ripped free to become sharp wind-borne missiles.

Attempting to capture the scene on film was terrifying, but for the wildlife the storm was devastating. Most of the forest creatures had literally gone to ground or were sheltering in the lee. Deer sought the safety of a young plantation, for it is the full-grown trees that are most vulnerable to storm damage. A pair of crows rode out the storm clinging to a wind-tossed branch, while nearby a tree that had formed the roof of a mouse's nest had been torn away leaving a mass of tangled roots. The full extent of death and disturbance to wildlife caused by a gale is seldom if ever known. Foresters only reckon the damage in terms of wind-thrown trees.

The gale raged without check for three days, doing most damage where recent felling had left clearings which acted as wind tunnels. These allowed the full force of gusts to reach the centre of the plantation, flattening large tracts of forest. Early on, when the winds were at their height, nature felled in minutes what would have taken a chainsaw gang several days to achieve. After the storm, more trees had to be cut and cleared by teams of foresters, before most of the fallen timber could be extracted from where it lay in a tangle of trunks and branches.

The action of wind has a more subtle effect beneath the ground. The more a tree is rocked by the wind, the faster its roots grow. Trees that are continually exposed to wind are shorter and thicker in girth than those in sheltered positions and also have a substantially larger root area. So the trees standing on the edge of a forest are better able to withstand wind than those inside. If a number of edge trees have been felled shortly before a severe storm, the rest of the plantation may be flattened.

Under constant storm-force winds, a tree bends gradually and suffers surprisingly little damage. Unfortunately, the wind is seldom if ever constant. During the more usual sudden gusts, the speed of the wind increases momentarily, followed by a brief lull, and the tree begins to sway. If the timing of subsequent gusts coincides with the frequency of that sway, the trunk gathers momentum, and bends with increasing violence, until the roots are ripped from the ground or the trunk snaps in two.

A few decades ago, commercial forests were planted so that all the trees matured, and reached a vulnerable height, at the same time. On the night of 14 January 1968, a fierce gale in Scotland felled about 1.5 million trees, an area larger than Loch Lomond. The hurricane which struck south-east England in October 1987, although felling some 15 million trees, caused far less damage to forestry plantations. This is partly because, in the intervening years, the threat of wind damage had become a major factor in determining what trees to plant and where. Today conifer planting is usually staggered so that as one small area of woodland is reaching maturity, another contains trees of mid-term growth. A patchwork pattern of growth not only reduces the danger of wind-thrown trees, but also benefits the wildlife which cannot flourish in the uniformly dense shade of mature plantations.

During the lengthening days of early spring, the conifers and the insect life they support become more active. The conifers' leaf buds have been protected from winter frosts within a sealed coat, surrounded by additional layers of dead tissue. Now they start to break through this seal and begin their new year's growth. The eggs of weevils and moths, laid inside the needles or beneath the bark in the previous summer, hatch in the morning sun to form a ravenous army of grubs and caterpillars.

Relatively few insect species thrive on conifers but those that do often occur in large numbers. The caterpillar of the pine beauty moth, well camouflaged by its lateral stripes, can threaten entire plantations. Larger, though generally found in far fewer numbers, are the caterpillars of the pine hawk moth. Small sawfly larvae consume leaves in groups of ten or more, while aphids suck the resinous sap. One kind of tiny adelgid insect produces strange gall-like growths, resembling miniature pineapples, on the tips of Norway spruce. Wood-boring beetles and their grubs tunnel a distinctive pattern of galleries beneath the bark along with weevil larvae, while the adult pine weevils seek out the bark of young trees to consume. One of the largest and most spectacular insects of the forest is the giant wood wasp or horntail, so called because of the long protruding 'sting' which extends from the female's rear. Far from being a defence, this structure is a harm-

An anting jay (*below*) is believed to be using the wood ants' spray as a cleansing agent to rid its feathers of parasites. *Opposite* Wood ants emerge in their thousands from winter hibernation (*inset*) and the old tree stump is soon covered as they build their enormous nest mound of leaves (*main picture*).

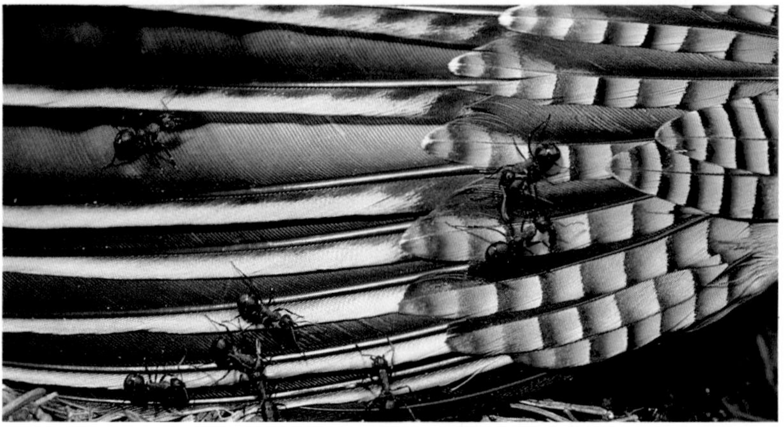

less ovipositor, enabling eggs to be laid deep in the wood of a dead or dying tree.

A period of settled, sunny weather in spring brought the pine trees of Haldon's plantation into flower. Male and female parts are borne separately at the tips of the shoots. The female flowers are small and insignificant tufts, sometimes red in colour. The much larger male flowers release immense quantities of wind-blown pollen into the air. Carried by the hint of a breeze, the bright yellow fertile clouds slowly swirl through the forest, pollinating the female flowers as they fall. The northern summers are too short for the cones of some species of conifer to mature in one year. Away from the tip, the tiny green cones of the previous year begin to swell. Further back on the branch hang the wooden brown three-year-old cones, now with widely splayed scales. Despite popular opinion, the cones do not predict but merely react to the changing weather. Controlled by moisture-sensitive cells at the base of each scale, the cones open in the warm dry weather to release a shower of tiny winged seeds to the wind.

One of the essential sounds of the plantation in spring, blending in with the background symphony of bird calls, is a repeated hammering echoing across the forested slopes. From close quarters I could see that the noise was produced by the great spotted woodpecker's beak striking a tree trunk in a series of rapid blows. These handsome, pied-plumaged birds with their coloured flashes of crimson red on the nape and under the tail, wing their way in deep undulating flight from one tree to the next. Now that spring had come they were turning their attention from the cone seeds that had been their diet in the winter months to the ever-increasing number of tree-boring grubs.

With two toes splayed forward and two more aft, a woodpecker clung to a vertical trunk. Its short stiff tail acted as a prop as it angled its body to absorb the resounding shock of its blows. It had chosen carefully a tree with some rotten wood, and used its acute sense of hearing to detect prey beneath the bark. Even beetle larvae make a noise when chewing their way through wood. Extracting the grubs in a similar way to the seeds of a cone, the woodpecker's strong, resilient bill penetrated the grubs' gallery, and the tongue licked out the prey. So long is the tongue that it is contained within a sheath which extends up and around the back of the skull ending inside the upper beak. The length only provides reach, and it is a barb at the end of the tongue which collects the meal.

The woodpecker's drumming also serves as a territorial claim, to attract a mate and, later, to fashion a nest. Any damage done to the bark of most conifer trees is quickly covered by exuding sticky resin. In addition, young forestry plantations lack trunks large enough for the bird to excavate a nest chamber. So woodpeckers tend to seek out more mature growths or surrounding hardwood trees in which to nest. There are few other birds that can produce a nest which is literally hammered home. When the woodpecker has abandoned its nest, the hole will be used by many different birds.

On the edge of a forest path I came across the remains of a rotten stump from which flowed a writhing black mass resembling lava spewing from a miniature volcanic mound. After their winter hibernation underground, millions of wood ants were being warmed into action by the increasing strength of the sunlight. Within hours, the ants began to repair their nest, replacing the material that had been washed away by winter storms. Over the following weeks, pieces of pine needles and leaf litter carried by an army of ants would be used to build up the nest – wood ant nests can be as high as one metre.

The home of a wood ant colony is an intricate system of tunnels and galleries permeating several levels beneath the surface, often built on a natural hump or around a rotten stump or fallen log. Larger chambers house the egg-laying queens and the nurseries of developing young. The nest is built at the edge of a clearing where it can be warmed by the sun. Together with the heat generated by the massed body of ants, this raises the temperature of the mound. In summer, the ants cool the nest by opening up passageways and vents, thus creating a microclimate all of their own.

Though made up of millions of individuals, the colony acts in a well-organised unified way. Every morning ants radiate out from the nest and up the trees. The wood ant workers appear not to lace their well-followed trails with invisible chemical scents as other species of ants do, but nevertheless find regular feeding grounds with ease – presumably by feel. They climb to the new growth right on the very tips of the trees, where the majority of aphids are found. Aphids are soft-skinned insects, seldom more than a few millimetres in length, with a narrow head and a bulbous body. They pierce the stem of a plant with a mouthpart tube, and drink the sap. The aphids seem to need copious quantities of sap in order to obtain enough nourishment, and in the process imbibe far more sugar and other sap products than their bodies can cope with. The excess passes straight through the digestive system and drops to the ground or onto the surrounding foliage. It is this sticky, energy-rich secretion, known as honeydew, which attracts relays of ants. The relationship between aphid and ant is a mutually beneficial one. While the wood ants gain a constant supply of food, their powerful jaws protect the aphids from predatory insects. The relationship is so close that where aphids are regularly attended by ants they will produce up to three times more honeydew than normal. It has been estimated that a single ant colony will collect an amazing 50 kg of honeydew in a year.

Opposite The floor of a conifer forest, carpeted in a thick layer of needles, supports little plant life – only fungi and bracken flourish here. *Below* The nightjar, feeding her chicks on a bolus of moths, is an uncommon bird that breeds in the clearings and early stages of forestry plantations.

Wood ants are highly efficient predators themselves, bringing back caterpillars and adult insects many times their own size to the nest. When foraging for prey, they follow no special trails and appear to find food merely by chance. If the prey is large, other ants are attracted by the activity, and help to drag it back, or to cut it into smaller, manageable pieces. However circuitous the path an ant has followed to find food, it always takes the shortest route home. Since wood ants forage even at night, the means by which they find their way back to the nest is something of a mystery. Each covers a small territory and so it is possible that the ant comes to know its area in sufficient detail to navigate using landmarks.

On a fine day, the area around the nest will be a frenzy of ants scurrying backwards and forwards in search of food, or cleaning out or repairing the nest. This busy activity may arouse unwelcome attention from the yaffle or green woodpecker. In flight, it appears as a flash of bright green with a laughing call while on the ground it is a large and rather ungainly bird. Its long, fast, probing tongue flicks through the tunnels of the colony, finding a ready meal of wood ants and their brood. However, the ants are not defenceless. Taking on the role of soldiers, some workers literally stand up to the intruder. They swing the tip of their abdomen through their legs and spray rapid bursts of formic acid at the bird. The woodpecker may beat a temporary retreat before returning to continue its feast.

Apart from woodpeckers, few birds can tolerate the acrid taste and defensive tactics of wood ants. The now rare wryneck is a specialist ant feeder, while the far more common pheasant takes its fair share, though it does not feed exclusively on ants. Other birds search out ants' nests for reasons far removed from food. Many passerine birds take advantage of the insecticidal nature of the ants' spray to cleanse their feathers of minute lice and mites. Starlings, rooks and thrushes have all been observed taking an acid shower, but the most frequent bather is the jay. It wallows in a pool of squirting ants as it performs a dance with its crested feathers raised, tail splayed and wings spread and drooped. Ants are picked up and held beneath the wings in fast and flurried succession. Never staying still for more than a few seconds, the jay prances on and off the nest. After the bath, it usually spends some time bathing, oiling and preening its feathers.

It was now April and the increasing warmth and longer days brought more creatures out from hibernation. Where an avenue of alder buckthorn broke the monotony of conifer trees, brimstone butterflies flashed their brilliant yellow wings. Overwintering as adults, they are among the first of their kind to fly the woodland paths in spring. As I watched, one of Britain's most common and only venomous snakes slid into the sun from between the twisted stems of a heather-clad hummock. Flattening its zig-zag striped body to expose a greater surface to the warming rays, the adder quietly curled itself round. The males emerge first from a winter spent deep below ground, followed within a few weeks by the females. Seldom more than 50 cm long, the adder gives the curious impression of being larger than it really is, perhaps because of the thickness of its girth compared with its length. The brown-coloured females are generally longer than the greyer males, but both have characteristic dark jagged markings down the back, especially vivid in spring after the first moult of the year.

Lizards make up a large part of the adders' diet and they will also take small mammals, frogs and newts. Once the immediate need for food has been satisfied, the major activity is to find a mate. Males will often fight in defence of territory, but their attention is easily diverted to the pursuit of a female. During courtship, they move in and out of cover, and may fall victim to predatory birds. The buzzard will not hesitate to tackle a large adder, which it grips firmly in long vice-like talons. The bird keeps the writhing reptile at legs' length, rendering the adder's venomous strikes futile.

Once the excitement of courtship and mating is complete, those that have not fallen prey to birds or even badgers, slide back to a more cautious solitary life. The adders feed regularly during the summer months building to a peak in the autumn, when a sufficient fat store must be acquired to sustain them during their winter hibernation. A breeding female must not only lay down a store for herself but also build up food reserves for the 5 to 20 young developing inside her. She will spend the summer hunting several hundred metres or more from her wintering grounds, and then return in August to produce her young. In common with all reptiles, the young adders develop in an egg. However, the mother retains the eggs within her body and so appears to give birth to live young. This protection is particularly important for the developing young in colder climes, but puts such a strain on the females that they can only breed every other year. The newly emerged snakes survive their first winter drawing on their inborn food reserves.

In the April sunlight the distant rasp of chainsaws rose and fell, as foresters thinned out a section of trees. Well away from the sound of human voices, a roe buck emerged from dense shade, ears twitching and head held high as it strutted hesitantly. Unlike most deer, the roe grows its antlers during the winter months and they were now covered in an outer layer of skin. The deer frayed this velvet against the branches of trees. It then began to mark out its territory by rubbing its head against trees and shrubs, depositing scent from a gland between the antlers, and scraping the base of the tree with its forefeet. Inevitably saplings are damaged by this behaviour, and shredded bark is a sign of the presence of deer. The buck will claim any doe whose range overlaps with his marked-out area.

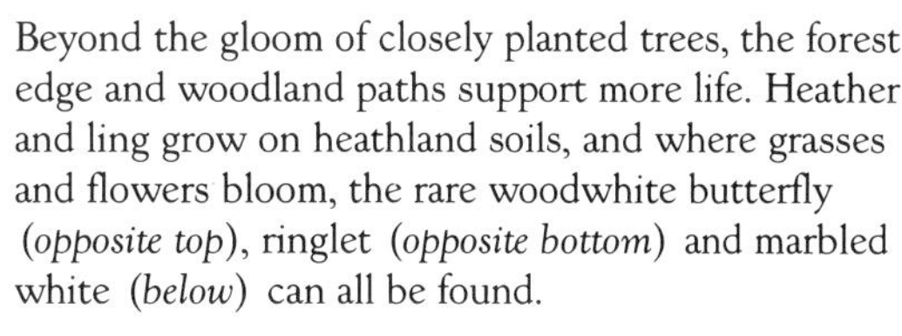

Beyond the gloom of closely planted trees, the forest edge and woodland paths support more life. Heather and ling grow on heathland soils, and where grasses and flowers bloom, the rare woodwhite butterfly (*opposite top*), ringlet (*opposite bottom*) and marbled white (*below*) can all be found.

The plantation also supports a number of fallow deer. More social than the usual solitary roe, the sexes gather in separate herds until the autumn rut. The smaller roe deer's rut begins considerably earlier in mid-July, but the young of roe and fallow deer, like those of red and sika deer, are born the following May or June. The reason lies in the roe's ability, unique among deer, to delay the development of the fertilised egg. At first, the egg grows slowly and remains free floating. By the end of December the embryo has implanted in the wall of the womb and is developing rapidly. Roe deer often give birth to twins, and single fawns; triplets are less common. The fawns have conspicuous rows of white spots from birth until they are around three months of age. When the young lie quite still surrounded by vegetation, the spots break up their outline and shape, making them very difficult to see from only a few paces away.

Late one afternoon at the end of May, a tiny movement stirred the layer of moss and dead needles at the base of a pine. A pine hawk moth was struggling to free itself from the soil, where it had overwintered as a pupa. With its wings still crumpled, its delicate legs pulled the bulk of its large trailing body up the tree. There it clung for several hours as its wings slowly unfurled. This handsome moth, found mainly in the southern half of Britain, feeds on flowers, especially those of the twining stemmed honeysuckle. The adult life of the moth is brief, varying from a few days to several weeks. During this time the female must find a mate and lay a scattering of small green eggs on new pine growth. The eggs hatch in July or early August, and the emerging larvae are not much broader than the needle leaves they consume. The caterpillars eat, steadily, slowly fattening themselves on some of nature's toughest leaves, until after several weeks and many moults they are finger-sized. In October they burrow into the ground and pupate over winter, to emerge as moths in the following year.

As the May sun sank between distant trees and the wind died to barely a breath, a truly remarkable bird appeared. The first hint of its entrance on the slopes of the forest clearing was a soft but insistent 'coo-ic'. The nightjar rose from the ground where it had spent the day and alighted on the arched branch of a solitary birch, spared by the foresters' saws. The bird sat along the branch, instead of crosswise like most other birds, and its first plaintive calls gave way to a continual 'churr'. The pitch changed abruptly as the bird turned its head to broadcast its territorial claim. A tawny owl taking to the air with a shriek caused the nightjar to fall silent and flatten itself against the branch. Tawny owls are not known to tackle a bird the size of a nightjar, but this one was obviously not taking any chances.

Once danger had passed, the bird resumed its strange call, with its distinctive profile silhouetted against a rising half moon. Only a little larger than a blackbird, the nightjar has a flat head with large eyes and a tiny bill. The long hawk-like wings and trailing tail are picked out in the male by brilliant patches of white near the tips.

Typically a bird of dry, sandy heaths with scattered trees, the nightjar has adapted to life in young plantations. At the end of the nineteenth century it was a common bird but it has since suffered a drastic decline. Today it is relatively rare with scattered strongholds throughout the British Isles, the main concentrations being in the south.

The nightjar feeds on the wing, snatching moths and other insects of the night in its wide gaping bill. Stiff bristles at the corners of its beak protect the eyes from the fluttering prey. By day the birds are seldom seen, for their mottled brown plumage renders them almost invisible as they lie motionless on the ground. If approached, their large nocturnal light-gathering eyes narrow to thin slits.

As suddenly and silently as it had arrived the nightjar left the branch and pirouetted on upturned wings, gliding gently towards the ground. Disappearing into the shadow below the line of trees, its call changed to a soft bubbling, punctuated by sharp claps of its wings. In a continuing cartwheel, it displayed above its mate and chosen nest site. The female nightjar had laid her two eggs in an unlined scrape in a tiny clearing near some dead wood. Shaded by a miniature forest of bracken fronds, she stayed quite still during the heat of the day. The temperature within the hollow can soar during the summer but these birds are no strangers to heat. They overwinter in Africa, south of the Sahara, returning to the same nesting area with the coming of each British summer.

After eighteen days' brooding, the eggs hatched out and the fast-growing fluffy chicks were fed by both parents during the night. Like their parents, they rely on their extraordinary camouflage to avoid detection. However, the young are vulnerable to being chilled, and gathering storm clouds and a distant roll of thunder drove them to shelter beneath their mother. The torrential rain soaked the soft forest soil, but the nest site had been chosen with care and the tiny rivulets and miniature flash floods passed the family by. After the downpour, the chicks shuffled out into the sun, while the female shook the raindrops from her back and dried out in preparation for her nocturnal foray. If all went well, the young would move to denser cover after the first week, and be flying ten days later. The parents would then rear a second brood in the same season.

A hot and sultry June day brought great activity among the wood ants, as winged adults emerged from the mound. In this culmination of the colony's year,

The hobby is a summer visitor to Britain where it occupies old crows' nests in tall trees. Although it is found throughout the country, it remains rare for, despite legal protection, the eggs are avidly sought by collectors and the parents and young birds then face an annual gauntlet of guns during their migration to tropical Africa.

the new queen ants and smaller males were leaving the nest to found new colonies. They had waited for the warm, gently rising air, which would aid their flight, before swarming to the surface. Unlike many other species of ants, the mating flights of wood ants are rarely if ever on a massive scale. The few hundred individuals mate on the wing or wherever they land. Many fall prey to insect-eating birds and, once mated, the males die anyway, their part in a future colony now being held by a queen. She may come to ground kilometres away or just a few hundred metres from her natal nest. Shedding her wings, she burrows her way into the needle-strewn soil to start a subterranean lifetime of egg-laying.

At first the queen ant feeds the grubs herself. As the young ants mature, teams of workers take over the tending of the nurseries and the queen. The smooth white, kidney-shaped eggs hatch into white hairless grubs which grow and moult several times. The workers produce a juice for small grubs by chewing and digesting prey with their own salivary fluid. The larger grubs can digest insect material themselves, and the nursery workers merely cut the prey into small pieces for them. The time taken for an ant to grow from an egg to an adult depends on the temperature and the availability of food. In established wood ant colonies, the queens and male grubs are usually reared early in the year when the weather is cool. The labour force of the colony is made up of infertile female ants which emerge during the peak season for growth, the summer. The younger workers tend the nursery, while the older worker ants forage for food and build up and defend the nest.

Like other conifer plantations, Haldon's plantation is laid out on regular lines, bisected by roads and foresters' tracks wide enough to accommodate the giant log-hauling machines. Criss-crossing the plantation are wide belts of cleared ground designed to limit forest fire, a constant danger in dry weather. There are even wider corridors below the huge metal pylons which keep the massive currents in power cables high above the ground.

Although their geometric precision may make them appear unsightly, all these clearings are a blessing to wildlife. The creation of a plantation, with great machines ripping into the topsoil and the subsequent growth of light-excluding conifers, destroys the habitat of many of our native wild flowers. The wide paths sweeping through the forest allow the sun to penetrate and enable a profusion of woodland and sometimes wetland plants to flourish. In the damp ditches beside the paths, early purple orchid spikes stood erect, soon to be drowned in a growing sea of grass. Sways of brambles bent out from scrub-covered banks and untidy pink and white dog roses littered the pathside.

A clearing felled the summer before provided a bright open space where foxgloves were recolonising long-lost ground. However, their dazzling purple display would be shortlived. Rows of young trees had already been planted and would outgrow the flowers in a year or two. It may be forty years or more before the slopes are again laid bare. Then the wind-scattered seeds of a few foxgloves which have survived along the woodland edge will fall onto the newly stripped ground, and the cycle will start again.

Accompanying this variety is a wealth of insect life. The woodwhite butterflies, delicate cousins of the larger and more common cabbage whites, are a local rarity whose caterpillars feed on trefoils and small vetches. The more frequently seen marbled white has chequerboard markings and a name which belies its inclusion in the family of brown butterflies. As the summer progresses, a succession of butterflies, from ringlets and meadow browns to fritillaries and speckled woods, emerge, adding to the colour of the flowers.

Nestling in a tree-lined hollow on the hillside, a purpose-built but now natural-looking pond attracts and sustains the area's wildlife. During the summer months, multi-coloured flocks of adult and young crossbills come to drink and bathe. Deer are early-morning visitors to the pool, and adders, too, take advantage of it in dry weather. With a bird-like action, the snakes take in a small quantity of water and then lift up their heads and allow it to trickle down their long throats.

A few weeks later, by mid-morning, the rising July heat had lessened the almost incessant hum of midges and flies. Dragonflies still skimmed across the dark surface of the pond, chasing each other or darting after insect prey. Then a chanting call broke the silence and a scimitar-winged shape appeared high above the trees. Plummeting on swept-back wings, the hobby twisted and turned before looping the loop and settling on the bare branch of a nearby tree. This high-speed acrobat will snatch a dragonfly in its claws and consume it while flying, and can even catch swifts on the wing. Its diet consists chiefly of large-winged insects, such as grasshoppers, and small birds and bats. The hobby's slate-grey back and fine black moustache markings resemble those of its close relative, the peregrine falcon. However, the hobby is smaller, and its more heavily streaked breast is set off by distinctive chestnut-coloured 'trousers'. It overwinters in tropical Africa and returns each year to the forests and heathlands of southern Britain to breed. Sadly it has become a rare sight, and there are only about 100 pairs currently nesting in this country. The hobby lays its eggs in a deserted crows' nest or sometimes a squirrel's drey. The young, usually a pair, hatch out in July, when an abundance of small birds can be found for food.

This hobby's white down-covered chicks lay on a platform of twigs built

Forestry plantations themselves support only a limited wildlife but the space created by felling allows plants such as the foxglove (*opposite*) to colonise the ground. *Below* The ground beneath electricity lines is kept permanently clear and here more plants, such as the dog rose and bramble, can thrive.

close to the top of a larch as high as a four-storey building. They instinctively kept low down in the nest while the female sat preening her long tapering wings on the branch of a neighbouring tree. A ringing cry announced the male's arrival with freshly caught food, and his mate flew out to meet him. Soaring and circling, she gained height as the male dived towards her. At the very last second, the birds twisted and, with talons barely touching, transferred the prey. Returning to the nest she tore the hapless house martin into more manageable pieces before feeding them to her waiting young.

By the end of August the young hobbies were on the wing, although still being fed by their parents. Within a few more weeks, they would be independent and undertaking their southward migration. If they managed to survive the dangers – including the guns of Mediterranean hunters – on their journey to Africa, they might return to breed the following year. Back in Britain, they would still be at risk from human predators. While the hobby is seldom shot at in Britain, its eggs are highly attractive to collectors, and, despite legal protection, many are stolen each year.

Forests are clearly far more than just a planted crop, and managing them with a degree of compromise adds to their diversity. In the past, the Forestry Commission has been criticised for practising monoculture on a vast scale, and for disregarding the area's wildlife. Today, its approach is far more sensitive. Among other improvements, native deciduous trees are being left increasingly around new plantations and planted along streams and paths. Indeed, it is now Forestry Commission policy for at least five per cent of new plantations to consist of deciduous trees. By adding to the diversity of plant life the nature of these areas is considerably enhanced. Even badgers, which traditionally inhabit broad-leafed woods, are to be found around many plantations, benefiting the foresters by consuming vast numbers of beetles and grubs.

People can wander around some mature plantations, and learn about as well as enjoy this enriched forest environment. Visitors are actively encouraged by the provision of visitors' centres, ample car parking, planned trails and picnic tables situated along suitable routes. Public access can cause problems, however, such as damage to plants, the theft of young trees near Christmas, and the poaching of deer. Even more worrying for the foresters is the increased danger of fire. Any prolonged period of rainless weather accompanied by drying winds makes the plantation more vulnerable.

This was demonstrated only too well in Haldon's plantation. For the second week in succession the skies dawned clear each day, and the unusually hot autumn weather had dried the grass verges of the forest paths and roads to a pale brown. Roe deer, followed by their spindly-legged fawns, came each dawn to drink at the steadily shrinking pool of fresh water. As the heat of the day intensified, a faint breath of wind stirred the stems of the rosebay willowherb. Their tall spires of pink flowers had bloomed throughout the summer and set seed. Now the pods were drying in the heat and peeling open to release millions of tiny cotton-tufted seeds. Drifting on the slight breeze, they rose in eddying clouds to fall in a scattered shower out beyond the trees. A busy stretch of straight road runs through the forest, linking the dual carriageway and a nearby village. A cigarette, carelessly tossed out of a car window, lay smouldering on the roadside. Another car swept past, fanning the flames so that they spread rapidly across the dry grass and up the bank. Once the fire had started, it crept steadily across the open ground flanking the road. The afternoon was so bright that the flames were almost invisible as they reached the forest edge, and only the tell-tale plume of smoke revealed the fire. Pine needles shrivelled and branches flared as the flames reached up and set the forest ablaze. The rising smoke alerted the Forestry headquarters and the road was quickly sealed off. An army of beaters advanced, while firemen sprayed water to hinder the fire's spread. Downwind, foresters with chainsaws sacrificed trees to create a firebreak.

After several hours of firefighting, the towering blaze was gradually brought under control. All around, the red glowing skyline and billowing smoke marked the course of the fire, now beginning to fade with the last of the light. The trees left standing had been stripped of all their leaves and many more were reduced to darkly glowing embers. Damping down could have taken many hours more, but a timely downpour extinguished the last smouldering branches with a hiss.

Morning brought a desolate scene of blackened earth and trees. A notice-board warning of forest fires lay half scorched among the charred trunks. If the fire had happened earlier in the year, when many birds were nesting, the toll of wildlife might have been far greater. Mammals and birds would have fled at the first scent of smoke, but countless insects and perhaps some lizards and snakes could have been consumed by the fire. Only those that sought safety by going deep underground might have survived.

Once the land has been cleared young trees will again be planted. In the meantime, seeds gently drifting in the breeze will take advantage of the temporarily bare ground. Among the first colonisers will be the rosebay willowherb – not for nothing is it also known as fireweed.

Compared to the time span of ancient woodland, where individual trees may come and go over hundreds of years, the life of a conifer plantation is short – an ephemeral forest that is here today and gone tomorrow.

CHAPTER 2

POOLS OF CLAY

The brilliant blue flash and piercing whistle could signify only one bird. The kingfisher settled on a lakeside branch, peering fixedly at a movement underwater. Suddenly it dived with electrifying speed and surfaced with a fish in a raised crown of spray. The kingfisher blue blurred as tiny wings lifted the bird back up onto its perch. Bobbing its head and quickly looking around, the bird began to stun its prey with a series of deft sideways blows to the branch. The roach impaled on the kingfisher's lower bill was flicked off and caught with a juggler's skill born of just a few months' practice, for this was the bird's first winter. It swallowed the fish headfirst, so that the backward-raked scales and fins slid easily down its throat, and then wiped the remaining few scales from its bill with a knife-sharpening action on the branch.

Clouds gathered overhead, dulling the sunlit sheen of the bird's brilliant colours. As the drizzle began the kingfisher sat digesting its meal. Looking at this scene it was easy to imagine myself in some remote wild place. In fact, this kingfisher's kingdom was a man-made lake bounded by a busy out-of-town shopping centre in the Bovey basin of Devon. Unseen and undisturbed, the bird flew low and fast to another waterside perch and the chance of another small fish.

The kingfisher belongs to an ancient family of birds, and probably hunted in this area long before people trod the Earth or waded in its fresh waters. Although the kingfisher's way of life has changed little over millions of years, the Bovey basin has altered dramatically, particularly over the past century. Lying hidden in the depths of south Devon, it has one of the richest and finest deposits of clay, the mining of which has become a major industry.

Some thirty million years ago, long before Britain broke off from the European landmass, this area was part of a vast primeval basin flooded by mountain streams. High in the hills hot acid gases and superheated steam issued from the ground, pushed by volcanic pressures through fissures in the granite crust. Vast quantities of felspar, contained within the granite, gradually decomposed under enormous heat and pressure. These were carried up from deep underground to form white powdery deposits of the natural chemical kaolinite, more commonly known as clay. Over millennia, clay was deposited throughout what was to become Britain's West Country.

Ball clay, named after the Devon word for a spadeful, was washed from its primordial deposit by the action of wind and rain. The clay gave a white colour to the rivers flowing down through primitive forests. Much was lost as most rivers wove their way to the coast and spewed their contents into the sea. However, a few faltered in their downward descent, impeded by the lie of the land, and a river of clay spread out. This slowed to form a large shallow lake, its turbid waters gradually clearing as the clay began to settle.

Eventually a lake surrounded by forest-filled swamps covered the area that was to become a Devon valley. Such inland waters, where layers of finely filtered clay particles gently drifted to the bed, were rare. In the course of its journey the composition of this remarkable mud had subtly changed. Most of the coarse material had been lost and some humus had been gained, adding to its plasticity and strength. Millions of years later, the special qualities of ball clay were discovered and the Devon deposits became highly prized by generations of potter's and other clay workers.

Once the great Armorican mountain range formed the backbone of the south-west peninsula. Today its rotting granite roots still rise in rugged outline as Dartmoor. It is a dramatic backdrop to the Bovey basin, set midway between the moors and the sea. In place of the large primeval lake lie scattered trappings of an industrial age. The Romans are thought to have first discovered and exploited Devon clay. After the empire's armies finally returned to Rome, the beds lay undisturbed for centuries. In the sixteenth century, Sir Walter Raleigh inadvertently revived an industry by starting the habit of smoking tobacco. The finest pipes were made of ball clay, and as the craze spread across the country the demand for fine clay increased. By modern-day standards, however, the amounts mined were small, making little or no impact on the area. It was not until the mid-eighteenth century, when Josiah Wedgwood started fashioning clay to make the finest pottery of the age, that the first balls of clay were dug on any scale. Since then clay extraction has grown enormously to meet worldwide needs.

In the early days open-cast pits were dug manually, which limited their size and depth. With the advent of modern machinery the scale and depth of workings grew. As I approached the rim of one of the largest clay works, a man-made crater of lunar proportions fell steeply away. Tiny figures moving around in the depths emphasised the staggering scale of the pits. Gigantic trucks trundled up a series of slopes with dust swirling in their wake. Below, excavators gouged the ground, digging back in time, for the lower the layer the older the clay. When the pit is eventually abandoned, the now dry bed of the prehistoric lake may once again be submerged.

Some of the richest deposits of clay, now known to be more than 200 metres deep, lie alongside the fast-flowing waters of the River Teign, fed by many small tributary streams and by the River Bovey. The rivers owe their existence to the elevation of the moors, where rainfall is high and blanket bogs constantly trickle into streams. In January, the River Teign was already swollen by heavy winter rain when increasing winds and stormy clouds brought another heavy deluge. As I watched, I could see the river rise, first lapping against the overhanging grass on a river bend and then creeping with increasing speed out beyond its original course. Washed-away silt had turned the torrent red-brown and broken branches raced along its length. The water seeped between the grass across level ground, filling and swirling into ditches and depressions. Gradually the grass disappeared beneath a new brown lake and still the river continued to rise. A line of wooden fence posts stood marooned, linked to dry ground by lengths of rusted wire. A solitary snail climbed up one post, just managing to keep pace with the steadily rising water. Withered tufts of grass hung limply from the upper strands of wire, marking the level the waters had reached the last time the river broke its banks.

It may have been floods such as this that turned the old open-cast pits into lakes and ponds. In more recent years, clay has also been taken from much greater depths in underground mines. When all the clay within reach of the main shaft has been extracted, the adit is closed. Then the ground above subsides, creating a series of shallow depressions. Floods fill these to form wetlands which attract large numbers of overwintering wildfowl.

Opposite Ball clay extracted from the Bovey Basin in south Devon (*inset*) is big business, yet the abandoned flooded pits (*main picture*) have become areas of national importance for wildlife. *Below* Reed mace, better known as bulrush, sheds its seeds in early spring and in this way colonises new ponds.

When ice and snow blanket the rest of the country, many birds head for the generally milder south and west. Fast-flying teal slide to a spray-thrown stop on the dark choppy water of the wetlands, while mallard and widgeon keep close to the banks among the shelter of the reeds. If they can evade the wildfowlers' guns, they may survive to another breeding season. Others seek refuge among people, the lure of free food overcoming their fear. Wildfowl gather on lakes which are the central feature of country park walks or a landscaped attraction for shoppers.

The search for clay has left a variety of pools and larger lakes scattered around the low-lying Bovey basin. Some are no more than a metre in depth, while others could sink a fifteen-storey building without trace. The history of these stretches of fresh water spans the Middle Ages to the present day. This is reflected in their names – for example, Stover Lake and Pottery Pond, Indio and Ugbrook, Trago Mills, Rackerhays and Bradleys, Little and Large. It is also reflected in the life which inhabits them. Some contain an incredible mix and diversity of aquatic life, while others are relatively poor. The natural history of three of the lakes is so rich that they are deemed sites of special scientific interest. Their variety of dragonflies and damselflies is particularly important, with twenty-four of the thirty-seven species known to breed in Britain occurring in the area.

Lowland lakes, particularly well-established ones, are among the richest of freshwater habitats in Britain. Fringed with an emergent jungle of plants and floating beds of leaves, the lakes and ponds of the Bovey basin form a haven for animals of all kinds. Water bugs and boatmen live alongside spectacular waterfowl. Diving ducks and great crested grebes search for nourishing weeds or small aquatic creatures from the mirror-smooth surface down to the markedly different environment offered by the lake bed. In the surface levels, where the sunlight is strongest, a single droplet teems with microscopic life. Plants grow in profusion down to about a metre, and then diminish along with the light. The murky depths harbour mainly crustaceans, aquatic insects and bottom-feeding fish. The wealth and scale of wildlife in many of the larger lakes has benefited from the introduction of fish. These have been managed for many years by local associations of anglers, and lure fishermen of every pursuit.

Only the keenest of ardent anglers ever see dawn breaking over their favourite fishing grounds. As I too watched, the surface shimmered with the first rays of sunlight below a gently swirling low-lying mist. In the middle of the lake a golden-tinged swan gracefully dipped its arched neck, encircled by sparkles from the fleeting crests of ever-decreasing ripples. Out of the sky descended a regular early-morning visitor – a heron gliding in on heavy, drooped wings. With trailing legs pulled forward and its long neck stretched out, it gave a few laboured flaps and landed on the lakeside. The heron briefly raised its fine black crest, ruffling its feathers from the long pointed beak to the end of the tail. Then it waded into the water on stilt-like legs and paused in the shallows, craning its neck forward as a fish caught its eye. Minutes went by as it remained frozen, waiting for another movement of its prey. The mist melted away with the growing light, allowing me to see the heron more clearly. Its only movement came from a single feather stirring on its back. Suddenly it lunged forward with the speed of a spear, and a large eel wriggled in the clamp-like hold of its beak. Wading back onto the bank, the bird tossed its head in an effort to swallow the writhing fish.

The demise of an eel marks the end of one of nature's most incredible journeys. Hatching deep in the Sargasso Sea, some 5000 kilometres from Britain's shores, the larval eel is carried by ocean currents across the Atlantic to the mouth of the River Teign. After two or three years at sea it changes to a tiny elver and begins a freshwater migration upstream in the company of millions of its kind. To reach waters with no obvious outflow, such as lakes or ponds, the eel may have been carried by flood or even made its way over land. Eels are extraordinarily tenacious and tough fish, able to withstand drying out for hours on end. Protected by a thick skin and narrow gill-slits, they can wriggle through grass with surprising speed, travelling mainly at night. In the lake, the elver grows into an adult eel. After four to fifteen years, those which survive have grown up to a metre long, and undergo another change to suit them for marine life. The eyes enlarge, the jaw muscles shrink and the head becomes markedly pointed. The back darkens above a silvery belly, and the gut reduces in size as the maturing eel ceases to eat. In autumn, the transformed eels migrate back down rivers into the ocean, and, possibly, across to the Sargasso Sea to spawn. This marks the end of their life, as they are assumed to die after spawning.

The cormorant, which occurs as much in fresh water as in estuaries or out to sea, also hunts eels and other fish. Almost reptilian in looks, these birds swim low in the water with most of the body submerged. Early in the year they can often be seen at dawn on some isolated branch, standing with neck crooked and wings spread in heraldic pose. Unlike other web-footed birds, cormorants do not coat their feathers in a waterproofing oil. This aids deep diving but has the disadvantage that cormorants must dry out when back on land. They have huge appetites and can catch surprisingly large fish – to the envy of human anglers, confined to the bank, who are trying to do the same.

Although it was still January, moist westerly winds over the past week had brought unseasonally mild weather. Heavy overnight rain, combined with the increasing temperature, had prompted the start of the frogs' annual migration

Main picture Winter flooding extends a lake into the surrounding wood, creating a swamp where frogs gather to spawn in the shallows. *Below* Newly hatched tadpoles remain on the spawn while growing their gills. External gills adorn the head of the young great crested newt (*opposite bottom*). All can fall prey to the pike (*opposite top*) which can consume fish up to half its size and even eats its own kind.

towards their spawning pools. By morning the pondside was full of small bulbous-eyed heads and the sound of the males' mating calls. When approached too closely, they ducked beneath the surface, slowly reappearing after a few minutes to continue their croaking chorus. The large masses of spawn bulging out of the shallows indicated that hundreds of frogs must have been involved in the overnight gathering, and there were many more still to spawn. At the height of spawning activity, male frogs will grab at anything that moves, including fish and even a human hand. These are usually released quickly, but fish are occasionally drowned by the clasp of a male frog's passion. The spawn-swollen body of a female is grasped from above in an embrace known as amplexus, which may last several hours. Horny pads develop on the male's thumbs during this season to help him maintain a grip which will only be relaxed when the eggs have been produced. Gatherings of adult frogs on such a scale are not without their risks. A splattering of white droppings around the edge of the pool and the remains of a speared frog were the only signs of a heron's early-morning feast. Many other predators, including foxes, badgers and mink, will take frogs if given the chance. So spawning seldom lasts more than a few days and then the frogs disperse once more until the following season.

The fertilised spawn from a pair of frogs consists of up to 3000 eggs. At first the spawn sinks to the bottom of the pond, but as the protective jelly absorbs water and expands it floats to the surface. Each fertilised egg is just a single cell. Within two or three hours of being laid, the cell divides into two, and then divides again and again at intervals of about thirty minutes. During the process of division, the size of successive cells becomes smaller so there is no visible growth. By the following day, the original egg has been transformed into thousands of minute cells, each with its own nucleus. Over the ensuing days, the multiplying cells of each egg gradually develop a complex organisation to prepare for the construction and growth of the embryo organs and tissue.

The mild weather ended as the wind shifted to the north. A layer of ice lay across even the largest lakes and snow blew in sudden flurries. On one of the recreational lakes, ducks and swans gathered by the footpath and bridge, preferring even white bread to nothing. On other ponds, where the birds were not used to people and their bags of free food, they stood a safe distance away out on the ice.

The unique properties of water protect the life in the ice-covered lake. Ice is lighter than water, and the first icy fingers form a solid sheet of ice which floats on the surface. The temperature above the ice can continue to fall while the water below remains a few degrees above freezing. The thicker the layer of ice, the better the insulation, enabling freshwater life to survive the harshest spells.

When I returned two weeks after the spawn was laid, the first tadpoles were wriggling free. At first they are vegetarian, feeding on algae, but as they begin to grow, so too do their appetites. They become omnivores, using their rasping mouthparts to scavenge for the remains of other freshwater creatures, and to attack and feed upon their own kind. Within a month a flap of skin covers the external gills. At seven or eight weeks of age, the tadpoles have fully developed hind legs and lungs, and must come to the surface to breathe air. It will be more than three months before they are finally transformed into froglets with tails. By the time the tail is finally absorbed and the miniature frogs are ready to leave the water, midsummer will already have passed. The millions of tiny insects that have emerged during the summer months will form their staple diet. Those which survive for three years will return as adults to breed.

Toads emerge from their winter hibernation within days of the frogs or a month or more later, depending on the weather. Frogs often spawn in shallow, even temporary pools and, although they will return to the same vicinity each year, they will not necessarily breed in the same pool. Toads prefer a deep-water pond or lake and will return faithfully year after year to the same place. Mild wet weather prompts the mass migration of toads to their traditional spawning ground. As dusk is beginning to fall, they crawl and occasionally hop from miles around. Their journey across fields and ditches, through woods and hedgerows, is for the most part hidden by the dark. Fallen trees or man-made obstacles must either be overcome or crawled around. This has the effect of funnelling huge numbers of toads through gates and along deep ditches. Where such channels lead onto busy roads, thousands of these slow-moving creatures are killed by passing cars. However, many more survive to reach the safety of deep water, and there the unattached males start calling in staccato croaks.

Some large spawn-swollen female toads arrive at the pond with a smaller male riding piggy-back, while others arrive on their own. Any small disturbance of the water causes the male toads to clamber over each other in anticipation of finding a mate. Caught in the centre of the amorous intentions of ten or more males, a female may even be drowned. The tumbling mêlée continues until a female and a mate manage to break free. They dive down to a depth of a metre or so, and any further advance by an unattached male is met with hefty kicks from the mated pair. The spawn is produced in a long string up to three metres in length, containing 300 to 7000 black eggs. The process is slow compared to that of the frog, taking many hours, but it is far less sedentary. The mating toads move through the water, entwining the string of spawn around weeds as they go.

After spawning, the toads gradually disperse into the surrounding

Opposite Herons nest in colonies high up in the tree tops. They breed early in the year and feed their young on eels, other fish and even frogs. *Below* The mute swan, once tamed and reared for food, today breeds successfully in the wild throughout Britain.

countryside until the following year. Like frogs, the mortality of young toads is especially high during their first few months. It will be four years before the toads reach sexual maturity and return to the same pond to breed.

Though less obvious in their gatherings, newts are almost as predictable in their choice of spawning pools as frogs and toads. The great-crested newt is the largest British newt, and also the rarest and most spectacular. After emerging from a winter hibernation spent under logs and stones, it assembles in traditional ponds. Within a few weeks the males have grown a jagged crest extending from behind the head down to the large tail. They are almost black on the upper surface, with a flash of brilliant orange marked with black spots on the belly. The females are similar, but lack the fine crest and are less brightly coloured.

The newts' courtship display is an elaborate aquatic dance in which the male takes the lead role. On the floor of the pond, he parades in front of his chosen mate before turning to face her. Then he releases an invisible scent and wafts it towards her by gently fanning and quivering the tail tip, occasionally lashing the entire tail. This is repeated until the female responds by following as he turns away. The male then deposits a white packet of sperm, called a spermatophore, in front of the female, and his part in the proceedings is over. She walks over this packet and picks it up in her vent, where the contents fertilise the eggs.

The female lays the eggs singly on the leaves of aquatic plants, and uses her hind legs to fold a leaf around each egg. This hides and protects them until they hatch about two weeks later. The newtpoles look very much more delicate than tadpoles and have three pairs of finely feathered external gills adorning either side of the head. The front legs of the newtpoles appear first, instead of the hind ones, as in frogs and toads. Four months later most of the young newts lose their external gills and begin to breathe air in preparation for a life on the land. A few remain in the water for another year, struggling to survive among their predators. Many different creatures, from the voracious nymphs of dragonflies and water beetles to young grass snakes and fish of every size, feed on tadpoles and newtpoles. Even a blackbird has been seen to stuff its beak with tadpoles and fly with its wriggling moustache to feed its nearby young.

At the end of March the level of the lake rose and water flooded the surrounding scrub. As I drifted in a small boat between the trunks of this seasonally submerged wood, large fish darted out of my way, leaving swirls in their wake. All fish have a sense organ – the lateral line – running the length of their bodies, which detects the slightest disturbance in the water around them. This enables them to feel the presence and distance of banksides, stones and other creatures, as well as an intrusive boat.

The most formidable predator of freshwater lakes is the pike. This powerful fish is well suited to life in rivers and lakes. Its dark green, torpedo-like body is dappled with yellow markings, camouflaging it as it lurks against a background of reeds waiting for passing prey. The pike's lateral line alerts it to the movement and position of possible prey such as another fish, a frog or even a young duck, before it can be seen. The large eyes, mounted high on its bony skull, give it a view of any meal passing above and ahead. The pike can move with incredible speed, covering ten times its body length in a second. Any prey grasped in its jaws stands little chance of escape. Needle-sharp teeth line the pike's lower jaw, while the entire roof of its mouth is armed with more than 1000 tiny ratchets, all pointing backwards.

Pike can live for many years and grow to a remarkable size, making them a valuable prize for anglers. Males may live for more than ten years, growing to a metre in length. Females can reach a length of a metre and a half and live for more than thirty years. As a pike becomes older and larger, it often starts to prey on its own kind. Its cannibalism makes the pike's courtship a risky affair. The huge egg-laden female moves up into the shallows and several smaller males may accompany her as she begins to spawn. The eggs are shed in portions over a period of three or four weeks, with the largest females producing over half a million eggs. While actually spawning, the female's predatory instincts appear to be suspended. However, as soon as the eggs are fertilised she may turn on her mate, repeating the performance a few days later with another luckless male.

The sticky eggs cling to plant leaves where they will be safe unless the spring floods recede early and leave them to die stranded. If they remain submerged and the weather is warm, the eggs will hatch in ten to fifteen days. The young pikes' mouths are not fully formed for the first few days after hatching and they survive by consuming their yolk-sac. Then they begin feeding on tiny planktonic animals before turning to aquatic insect larvae, crustaceans, the fry of smaller fish and tadpoles. When only twenty-five millimetres long, the young look like miniature adults, and they grow rapidly. Even so, the males take up to two years to mature while the females can take up to four.

With the arrival of warmer weather, the flooding of surrounding meadows began to dry out and, despite the odd shower, the lake slowly returned to its familiar shape. On an April morning, many of the most visible inhabitants of the lakes, the waterbirds, had started breeding and from the bankside scrub birdsong filled the air. But the peace was shortlived. A furious fight erupted out on the water. With long legs, white beak and white shield on the forehead, the rotund black coot is one of the most distinctive and aggressive residents of the lake. A

Opposite Coots are only sociable outside the breeding season, but both parents incubate the eggs (*bottom left*) – unlike the mallard (*bottom right*), which manages alone. *Below* and *bottom left* a moorhen chick, showing its egg tooth and clawed wing, feeds within hours of hatching. *Bottom right* The dabchick builds a floating nest of weed.

pair of coots held their heads low and wings raised in threatening posture as one coot invaded the territory of another. Threats soon gave way to a fight when the intruder did not retreat. Although their sharp beaks are formidable weapons, coots tend to launch into attack feet first. A fighting pair can often be seen with toes interlocked as they sit back in the water for a short while, before resuming the fray. Females, too, will join in; and even adjoining territory holders will become caught up if the battle spills over into their part of the lake. This fight ended almost as abruptly as it had begun, the intruding coot beating a retreat across the water, pursued by the victor. Coots defend their nesting areas so jealously that they will even attack moorhens and ducks.

While coots prefer large open areas of water, the smaller closely related moorhens appear to thrive in little more than a water-filled ditch. Although their name is a corruption of mere-hen, meaning bird of the lakes, moorhens occur mainly around the water margins. Black like coots, they are easily distinguished by their red forehead and white under-tail flashes, which are frequently displayed in courtship. During winter, the birds feed in small flocks on open ground near water, and then in the spring they begin pairing before setting up a territory. Moorhens tend to be faithful to one mate but, unusually among monogamous birds, it is the females that play the leading, often aggressive role in courtship. The females fight by striking with clawed toes and the largest get the pick of the males. Their choice, rather surprisingly, is for the smallest males, which appear to have the advantage that they need less food to put on comparatively more fat. So small males can spend less time feeding and more time incubating the eggs. Moorhens and coots feed mainly on the vegetation found around the lakeside or underwater. The coot especially dives to collect aquatic plants and returns to the surface to feed. Both birds also consume insects, worms, snails and fish, and coots will take the eggs of other waterbirds.

Some species of birds are limited to lakes of a certain size. For example, the great crested grebe needs an area of fresh water large enough to allow for its long take-off run and deep enough to allow it to dive for food. These birds are thus restricted to only two lakes in the Bovey basin and they frequent few other locations in the West Country. However, across the country as a whole, grebes have taken to many man-made stretches of water.

The great crested grebe is an attractive and striking bird, with its double-horned crest and chestnut frills about the head. Unfortunately, during the last century, it was almost exterminated in the name of fashion. The crest feathers, and sometimes the entire plumage, became popular decorations for women's hats. In 1857 the birds began to be massacred across England, and after three years they had become exceedingly rare. It is thought that there were just thirty-two pairs in the entire country, surviving on private and inaccessible lakes. New bird protection laws in the 1870s helped the grebes to recover their numbers, and they are now widely spread across Britain.

These birds are particularly exciting to watch during the breeding season, for they have a spectacular courtship. Their ceremonies can be seen from midwinter when the birds begin forming pairs and establishing territories. The males and females mirror each other in an extraordinary series of postures and displays. The most common is head-shaking, in which they meet beak to beak, with heads held high, and shake their down-pointed bills from side to side. Colourful names have been given to their other performances, including ripple dives, fish offering, patter flying and cat display. One of the most fascinating to watch is the penguin dance, in which the birds head-shake and then dive to collect some weed. After surfacing and swimming towards each other, they rise breast to breast from the water, vigorously paddling their feet and swaying their weed-filled bills from side to side.

The nest, built by the male and female, is a floating raft of vegetation, anchored to growing plants or the rising bare branches of some long-submerged shrub. The female lays three to five white eggs, and the attractive striped chicks are tended by both parents. The brood leave the nest soon after hatching and can often be seen riding on one adult's back while the other brings them food. This is not a joy-ride but a survival strategy, for it keeps the chicks warm and close to the best food supplies, and protects them from predators such as pike. After ten weeks the young are independent, and feed on a variety of small fish and molluscs, waterweeds and other vegetable matter.

The largest lakes in the region also support one of the largest birds in Britain, the mute swan. Like the grebes, this elegant bird's choice of water is limited by its pattering take-off run. In many species of monogamous birds, the fidelity is to a place rather than a partner. They return to the same nest site each year, and so stand a good chance of refinding their last mate. Swans, however, mate for life and the pairs form a close bond.

The territory of a pair of swans often covers an entire lake and they will defend it against any other swans. The appearance of another male causes the resident male to adopt a threatening gesture, swimming strongly with white wings raised in an arch over his back. If the unwelcome visitor does not leave, the resident male will launch an attack. Swan fights are dramatic affairs, with massive wings beating hard and sending spray high into the air. Fights between two strong swans can be prolonged and usually end with one opponent apparently

Between the pools lie the wetlands, water meadows and damp pasture which produce a lush display of wild flowers. The ragged robin (*below* and *main picture*) and several species of orchid, which can take several years to grow from a wind-blown seed to spectacular bloom, thrive in such places. The southern marsh orchid (*opposite top*) flowers from mid-summer, while the rarer green-winged orchid (*opposite bottom*) flowers in April–May and grows on drier ground.

attempting to drown the other by holding its head underwater. One fight I watched continued for nearly an hour until the intruder made a break for the bank with the resident bird swimming in pursuit. The beaten male then lay on the shore with its neck and head draped around its body. It remained there motionless for half an hour while the victor stood over it, preening its own battle-pulled feathers. Eventually the intruder made a hasty retreat to the far side of the lake and escaped.

If a male is injured or dies his mate is unlikely to be able to hold the territory on her own. A pair had held one of the lakes and reared broods successfully on it for several years. The female was in the final few days of incubating her eggs when the male was found dead. Only three out of the five large grey-green eggs hatched out. A week later, two of the cygnets had been killed by another pair of swans staking a claim to the lake. Without her mate's protection, she finally lost the third cygnet and left the lake.

Mute swans are large, imposing birds when fully grown and have few, if any, natural enemies, yet many are killed each year. Some, especially immature birds, collide with overhead power and telegraph lines. Nest sites are at risk from people who, wilfully or accidentally, disturb and even destroy them. A far greater number of swans suffer, and sometimes starve to death, after becoming entangled in or swallowing anglers' thoughtlessly discarded fishing tackle. Far more insidious is the effect of the tiny lead shot used by freshwater fishermen to weight their lines. While feeding on waterweeds in the shallows, the swans can consume large amounts of the shot, which slowly poisons them. As a result, many angling clubs now insist that their members use only stainless steel weights.

During the first really warm days of early summer, the air was filled with drifting white tufts as the alder trees lining the lake shore shed their seeds to the wind. The same southerly breeze had carried the flocks of swallows and house martins which now swooped low over the water, catching insects.

Around the actively worked clay pits and the lakes are wetlands containing meadows and streams, water-filled ditches and impenetrable woody scrub. They are often bounded by huge grass-covered ramparts, which act as screens and prevent premature flooding of any works. Closed to public access, these areas are seldom disturbed, and the wind-rustled reed beds resounded to the song of warblers, while the poker-like flowering parts of the bulrush grew proud of the emergent growth. Animals abound in the wetlands, including some unexpected inhabitants. The harvest mouse, with its long prehensile tail, is the smallest rodent in Britain. It was once thought to be restricted to farmland, but is now known to be more widespread. Harvest mice can be seen clambering among the close-growing stems of reeds and other wetland plants, in what may have been their original home. Before people started to farm, the only lowland parts of the country not covered by trees were the swamps, rivers and streams.

The fresh green of new leaves covered the trees and adorned the banks and water's edge. In the surrounding fields the grass stood tall, hiding a spectacular flora. One of the earliest plants of moist meadows to flower is the green-winged orchid. In common with a host of wetland plants it is becoming increasingly rare as more and more land is drained. The following weeks brought a colourful succession of flowers, including a yellow carpet of buttercups, the finely divided, rose-coloured petals of ragged-robin, and the knee-high purple spikes of marsh orchids.

As the bankside flowers bloom, so too does the luxuriant growth within the lake itself. The feathery-leaved water milfoil produces tiny reddish-green flowers which grow tightly around the stem just clear of the water. Many other plants, like the delicately flowered water violet, also grow submerged, only raising their blooms above the surface to be pollinated by wind. The Canadian pondweed, on the other hand, relies on water to carry its pollen. This bottom-rooted aquatic plant bears translucent leaves in whorls of three or, more rarely, four and, in its native home, male and female flowers. The male flowers break loose and float to the surface, where the stamens explode, releasing pollen. This drifts to the female flowers, which grow up to the surface on elongated stems. In Europe the male flowers are virtually unknown and the pondweed multiplies mainly by fragmentation of its extremely brittle stems. Canadian pondweed was originally introduced to Britain in the mid-nineteenth century where it flourished so fast that it soon became a menace to boating, fishing and swimming. After several years, however, it began to decline and it is no longer a serious problem. Indeed, it benefits the life of lakes and ponds through the streams of tiny bubbles that can be seen in sunlight emanating from its leaves. The Canadian pondweed is a rich source of oxygen for aquatic animal life.

The foliage of water plants also provides cover for fish and other creatures. Among the largest are the dinner-plate-sized flat leaves of the white water-lily. This plant lives in fairly deep water with its strong, rooting rhizome anchored in the muddy bottom, and its large leaves and waxy flowers held up to the surface on long stalks. The floating leaves provide shade and shelter in hot, sunny weather for frogs and newts, and landing platforms for dragonflies, damselflies, beetles and other insects. The undersides harbour jelly-like masses of snails' eggs and the firmly attached eggs of aquatic insects. The white water-lily's leaves are adapted to life afloat. Their tough waxy surface helps to prevent the leaves

Beyond the reach of fishermen lies a secret flower garden. The white water-lily (*below*) floats serenely in huge rafts, its large leaves supporting dragonflies and providing shelter for fish. The pink pondweed or amphibious bistort (*opposite, bottom left*) grows equally well both in and out of the water, while the fringed water-lily (*opposite, bottom right*) is strictly aquatic. Marsh marigolds (*opposite top*) grow around the pond edge.

becoming waterlogged. Oxygen and carbon dioxide from the air above pass in and out through stomata which only occur on the upper surface. The thin-walled underside allows gases and salts to be absorbed from the water below. The white water-lily's flowers can be spectacular, reaching up to twenty centimetres across. They only open on fine days and always close up at night. Each has up to twenty-five pointed petals arranged spirally around a centre of brilliant yellow pollen-bearing stamens. The flowers do not produce any nectar, but the warmth of the floral bowl, heated by the reflected rays of the sun, and the flower's perfume attract insects of many kinds, including beetles and small flies. Pollination occurs as the insects scrabble and even consume some of the stamens. The fruit of the lily is a spongy green berry which grows underwater and splits to release as many as 2000 seeds. These contain air spaces within their walls making them buoyant and they rise to the surface and disperse by floating away.

While many water plants are widespread, few thrive in the nitrogen-deficient ponds in which the greater bladderwort can be found. This curious free-floating aquatic weed supplements its nitrogen supply by consuming animal life. It has beautiful golden yellow flowers held clear of the water surface. However, the secret of its carnivorous habit lies submerged in the tiny bladders, little more than three millimetres in length, borne on thread-like leaves. Each bladder has an opening at one end covered by an inward-opening hinged door. Several stiff bristles, known as the trigger hairs, project around the opening, forming a kind of funnel. When an animal touches one of the trigger hairs, apparently attracted by mucilage glands near the entrance, the trap door opens and water rushes in, carrying the creature with it. The door snaps shut and traps the water flea or another creature of similar size, which dies and decomposes. The inner surface of the bladder is lined with glandular hairs which digest and absorb the animal's liquid remains.

Many underwater animals also feed by sucking in water, including the largest freshwater shellfish, the swan mussel. This bivalve mollusc has two hinged shells, or valves, closed by powerful muscles. In common with other molluscs, such as snails, the shell is secreted by a fold of skin, known as the mantle, covering the whole of the soft body.

The swan mussel usually lies half buried in the lake bed and has only limited powers of movement. If overturned or covered with silt, it will shift position using a muscular foot which is extended from between the shells. It feeds and breathes by extracting small food particles and oxygen from the water. A system of siphons draws water in through a tube and over a complex array of curtain-like gills. These remove the oxygen and trap food, which is transported on a conveyor belt of mucus, powered by cilia, towards the mouth. The filtered water is exhaled through another tube.

The hard shell is made up of three layers, mother-of-pearl, calcium carbonate and a horny layer of protein outside. Although inert, the shell is produced continually, increasing in size up to 150 millimetres long as the animal grows. The multi-coloured gleam of mother-of-pearl coating the inside of the shell is only revealed after the mussel's death. This inner layer encapsulates any foreign bodies, forming the tiny, often irregularly shaped pearls sometimes found in freshwater mussels. There are few, if any, natural predators capable of tackling the tough shells of full-grown swan mussels. However, the young miniature mussels, produced in the spring, are more vulnerable. They swim by clapping their two valves together until they locate a fish and bind onto it using sticky threads. The young mussels burrow into the fish's skin and feed on its blood, until they are about three months old. Then they leave the fish and settle down on the lake bed to spend the rest of their lives filtering water.

Dragonflies and damselflies adopt a much less passive style of feeding. These insects spend two or three years underwater as predatory nymphs, catching prey ranging from water fleas to small fish. Relying on stealth and camouflage in the hunt, nymphs lie in wait for a potential meal to pass within reach of their extendible mask. It has terminal hooks and, when not in use, the mask is folded back under the head. The nymph strikes with incredible speed, impaling its prey on the mask but causing only a slight stir in the surrounding mud.

In midsummer, the full-grown nymphs transform into winged adults, taking the hunt from underwater up into the air. I have watched this process many times, yet each emergence seems more extraordinary than the last. The nymph comes to the surface and clings firmly to a support, such as the stem of a water plant, twig or stone, with its head just clear of the water. Dragonflies emerge under cover of night, while damselflies, which take less time to complete their transformation, usually appear in the early hours of morning. During emergence the nymph is vulnerable and, if disturbed, it will retreat beneath the surface, reappearing after a few minutes. In some species the eyes slowly turn from brown to yellow. The nymphal skin splits behind the head and the adult slowly pulls itself free. At first, the wings are soft and crumpled, and hang free of the body. As blood is pumped through the tiny veins, the wings begin to spread out until all four lie flat. The newly emerged dragonfly hardens and the body assumes some colour until, a few hours later, it is ready to fly. However, several days pass before it attains its full brilliant colours, with wings that glint in the sun.

There are two main groups of dragonflies, the darters and the hawkers. Both

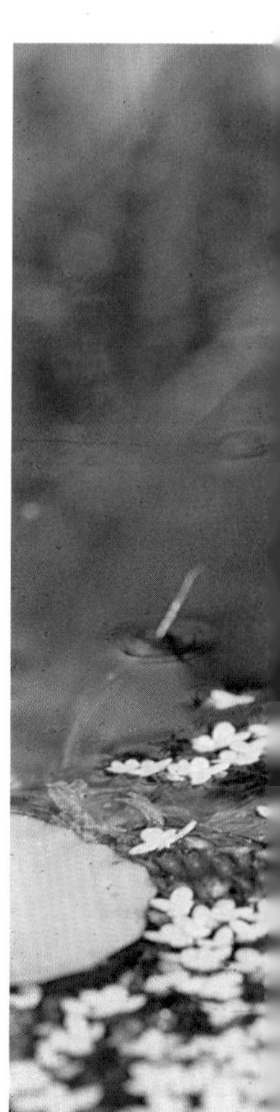

Opposite A hawker dragonfly has emerged overnight, leaving its nymphal skin still clinging to the stem of a reed. *Below* After mating, this female carefully lays her eggs inside a plant stem. The bladderwort (*bottom left*) is a carnivorous, free-floating plant. The swan mussel (*bottom right*) is the largest freshwater mollusc in Britain.

catch and consume small flying insects and are distinguished by their pattern of flight and their method of catching prey. The stout-bodied darters repeatedly dart out from some favoured perch, while the larger, more robust hawkers beat back and forth along a regular route.

For much of the summer, other colourful inhabitants of the lakes, the kingfishers, are often conspicuous by their absence. The river levels drop in summer and the streams form slow-moving clear pools, where there are plenty of small fry to feed a kingfisher's hungry brood. So from April onwards they nest in river and streamside banks and make only infrequent visits to the lakes. A pair excavate the fine sandy soil of a steep bank, carving out a tunnel nearly a metre in depth. The tunnel slopes up from the entrance to a small chamber, where the female lays her clutch of up to seven, almost round, glossy white eggs.

The chicks hatch within hours of each other between nineteen and twenty-one days after laying. White egg shells bobbing downstream or being carried by a kingfisher are signs that the young have hatched, for the parents quickly remove the pieces of shell and drop them some distance away from the nest. The need to remove the shells so promptly is difficult to understand. Many birds do so to keep their nests tidy, but the kingfisher's nest chamber is soon littered with the stinking remains of fish bones.

At first, the young are naked, blind and helpless. At one day old they appear heavy-headed with the beginnings of an oversize bill, and lean against each other as they struggle up at a parent's approach. The parents share in rearing the young, one flying off fishing while the other one broods. When one adult returns with food, it calls the other off the nest before entering. Initially the young are fed on small fish, and as they grow so too do their meals. Even fish which appear longer than the chicks themselves are swallowed headfirst in a series of gulps and soon digested. The bones and scales are regurgitated in a pellet. Excrement is propelled with considerable force towards the source of light. The slope of the tunnel helps the excrement reach the tunnel mouth and so keeps the nest dry.

Each chick can take up to eighteen fish a day, depending on the size. So each day the parents must catch more than 120 fish for a brood of seven, and about thirty more to satisfy themselves. By the end of the second week the brooding has stopped and both adults are hunting fish. As the young birds grow, the parents can no longer turn around inside the chamber and must leave the nest in reverse, tumbling back out of the hole. The nest becomes so foul that, after leaving it, the adults will sometimes plunge straight into the stream for a bathe. At this stage the call of the young is an incessant high-pitched churring, quite unlike the whistling call of the adults. At around three weeks of age the churring ceases and the chicks begin to utter a single 'chip' note. When they are between twenty-three and twenty-seven days old, the fledglings leave the nest and fly to a nearby branch, gaining their first glimpses of the outside world. The fact that they have been crowded together inside the nest chamber, with little room for energetic exercise, makes their initial flight all the more remarkable. They collect on a suitable branch, where they continue to be fed by their parents for a few days until they are able to fish for themselves.

By this time the young are almost identical to their parents, except that they have dark feet and a white tip to the beak. The beak also distinguishes the sexes in the adults being black in the male and having an orange flash on the lower bill in the female. They are spectacular birds, particularly when viewed at arm's length from behind the cloth of a canvas hide. At such close quarters it is surprising how small kingfishers really are, measuring just 16.5 centimetres from the tip of the beak to the end of the stubby tail. Lying in an average human hand, an adult bird would barely reach from the fingertip to the wrist.

Adult birds consume not only small fish, such as sticklebacks and minnows, but also a variety of other aquatic life, including dragonfly nymphs and water-beetles. They need clear and unpolluted water in order to catch their prey. If local streams and rivers swell, becoming turbid with heavy summer rain, chicks may go hungry as their parents make long flights to clear water ponds. Even worse, flood water can fill the nest, drowning the chicks inside.

Human disturbance also takes its toll. People may unwittingly remain too close to the nest, preventing the parents from returning with food. Some authorities straighten and grade waterway banks, which can bury nests beneath tonnes of excavated earth. Despite being legally protected, many kingfishers die this way each year. Severe winters also deplete their numbers because conditions prevent the birds fishing. Only one or two young from each brood may survive a harsh season to breed the following year. Luckily, kingfishers appear to recover their numbers rapidly after a bad year, often raising two, and sometimes even three, broods in a single season. One particular pair dug a second hole, and the female was incubating eggs, within three days of the first brood having successfully flown.

In common with all other natural features, ponds and lakes are always slowly changing. Their usual fate is to disappear gradually as silt and vegetation encroach from the sides into the centre. Then the swamp takes over, leaving no open water for aquatic life to flourish in. Animals that can fly or move over land must leave or perish. The plants that disperse by wind-blown seed will live on wherever they reach fresh water. Others, like duckweed, may be carried on the

Below The dazzling plumage of the kingfisher should make it a conspicuous bird but, being small, shy and fast-flying, it is seldom seen. An orange flash on the lower bill is the mark of a female. *Opposite* This fish's-eye view of a kingfisher on a rod gives an unusual perspective.

feet or feathers of wildfowl or on the boots of anglers to other ponds.

The stages in the natural succession of a pool are most evident around the edges of shallow, gently sloping ponds and can be seen in the distinct bands of plants, each of which is adapted to grow in a particular depth of water. It is possible in a human lifetime to witness the death of a small pond as the nature of the land succeeds that of water. Even the largest lakes are slowly vanishing, but on a time scale counted in centuries rather than in years. Indeed, such was the fate of the great lake that once filled the Bovey basin. A markedly different change awaits its smaller man-made successors. Beneath some of the largest and oldest complex of ponds lie layers of untouched clay. Workings were abandoned at what today is considered a shallow depth. These will be mined again in the next century as surely as the demand for the finest of ball clays will continue. Other old ponds have already been transformed. Water is first drained by massive pumps and the fish that remain are netted for transfer to fresh waters. Within days, dead and dying vegetation litters the shallow margins of the pit and sticky grey walls, now bare of life, plunge steeply into the silt-covered depths.

A valley of pits and pools, whether by accident or design, contains a valuable store of wildlife as well as clay. However, the speed of modern mining operations allows few creatures, apart from mammals and birds, to escape before the first excavators arrive. Individuals may perish but species will survive provided other suitable pools are within reach. Such pools could be purpose built and, given a long lease of life, would become natural reservoirs for plants and animals to survive and colonise new ponds. Exhausted pits could be backfilled with spoil from fresh mines, converting deep steep-sided works into the shallow gently sloping ponds so attractive to wildlife.

The natural history of the Bovey basin is not confined to the lakes and ponds. An industry that owes its origins to a primeval lake has inadvertently created a rich wetland in its wake. Where ponds were due to be destroyed, some effort has been made to move wetland plants and animals to a specially created reserve. It is even possible to move an entire meadow, along with its orchids and other plants, a turf at a time before the bulldozers arrive. The ability of wetland wildlife to survive annual floods and the rarer droughts enables it to cope with the long-term cycle of the birth and eventual overgrown death of a pond. Given time and a chance, it will continue to thrive.

The return of the kingfisher to a favourite perch, overhanging a quiet corner of the lake, marked the end of the summer months. During its absence, many of the surrounding small ponds had dried and the level of the lake had slowly dropped, revealing more of its mud and weed-covered banks. The resident swans swam serenely across the smooth surface as gathering dark clouds heralded a storm. A flash of lightning disturbed several large fish, which had been basking just beneath the surface concealed by water-lily leaves, and with a quick flip of their tails they were gone. As the thunder rolled overhead, the wind began to blow and the rain fell. The vital element that first washed and transported the clay, all those years ago, now submerged it once again in this valley of clay pools.

CHAPTER 3

STEAM AND WILDLIFE

On an early April morning in an old railway yard, smoke seeps from the roof of an engine shed. A pied wagtail flies from rail to rail until startled by a white hissing cloud that soon envelops the building. From the billowing mass, a huge familiar shape slowly emerges. A steam engine gleaming in the sun rolls steadily forward, its enormous wheels coming to a standstill as it vents once more. Weighing nearly sixty tonnes, it is a small tank engine by steam standards. Yet it is capable of moving several times its own weight, and is typical of the trains that left a smoky trail along country lines a century ago.

Powered by water under heat and pressure, the steam engine was once the wonder of the age, and the changes it brought to the British countryside were dramatic. Over a period of less than sixty years from the turn of the nineteenth century, the coming of the railways reshaped the landscape. A railway needs to be relatively level, rising or falling no more than waist high in a mile, and to be as straight as possible. So cuttings were gouged, vast embankments thrown up, tunnels dug and bridges and viaducts built by navvies, named after the navigators that built the canals before them. These men constructed the route and laid the track, helped only by horses. The scale was staggering, with some twenty tonnes of earth shifted each day at the height of the railways' creation. Not since the construction of the earth ramparts around huge hillforts in the Iron Age had the countryside witnessed such movement of rock and soil. The buildings of viaducts and bridges rivalled the construction of aqueducts in Roman times.

Isambard Kingdom Brunel was the architect of some of the railways' greatest structures, including the monumental stone viaduct over the Avon, and the elegant timber-framed viaducts spanning the steep valleys of Devon and Cornwall. The building of Brunel's Great Western Railway cut an almost level swathe, ten metres wide, from London to Bristol. Few lines equalled his broad-gauged track steaming up the Thames valley, passing through Reading and Didcot, and skirting the Berkshire Downs, before plunging into the darkness of Box tunnel. From there it crossed Bath on a castellated rampart before descending into the Avon valley and arriving at Temple Meads station in Bristol. Where it was considered too costly to dig or tunnel, explosives were used. It took nearly 120 tonnes of gunpowder just two minutes to level a 115-metre-high cliff during the construction of the South Eastern Railway in Kent. By the end of the 1850s, the transformation of the country was complete, and a railway network spanned and wove its way across Britain. An entirely new feature had been created along which the commerce of the country flowed, the life blood of an industrial age.

In 1825 George Stephenson opened the Stockton and Darlington Railway. It was the first line in the world to carry passengers, and for the next 100 years the railways had their heyday. Towns along the routes prospered and grew, and new towns, such as Swindon, sprang up. Platforms and stations, offices and hotels sometimes overshadowed their surroundings. Yet the railway also brought the countryside into the towns. Wildlife returned along the grass-lined margins of the lines. The wild flowers, which grew in profusion in the fields flanking the track, began to spread along the lines.

A plant which once thrived along railway lines is the yellow-flowered Oxford ragwort. This plant grows on the lava slopes of Mount Etna and was introduced to the Oxford Botanic Gardens in 1699. The ragwort spreads by releasing masses of feathery seeds to the wind. It escaped from the Gardens, and grew on city walls before reaching the Great Western Railway track in 1877. There it quickly colonised the clinker ash that so closely resembled its volcanic origins in Sicily. Soon the ragwort could be found all over the country, literally following in the wake of the trains.The movement of the trains drew its seeds into the slipstream and even into carriages, where the seeds could be carried for several kilometres before being blown out again.

The foundations for a railway line built on level land generally consist of a layer of cindery material, the clinker, over which the track bed or ballast is laid. The ballast is composed of large stone chippings and provides a firm, well-drained bed for the sleepers which support the steel rails on top. In modern sleepers, durable moulded concrete has replaced timber, which eventually rots. Most limestones were considered suitable for ballast, but, ironically, they soon began to break down under concrete sleepers, and greater use is now being made of granite. If the ballast becomes clogged with plant remains and oily waste from the trains, drainage will be impeded. This will lead to reduced support of the track, and eventual softening and failure of the subsoil below. For this reason the track must be kept clear of plant growth.

In the early years of the railways, regular maintenance of the track was carried out by lengthmen who worked up to seven in a gang. They removed plants from the track bed to stop it becoming clogged with weeds. They also cut back the rampant growth along track sides to give train drivers a clear line of sight and to reduce the fire risk. Grass fires caused by sparks from a passing engine were a constant threat during periods of dry weather. Sometimes fire became a tool rather than a threat, and banks were set alight to control brambles and scrub. The appearance of the line became a matter of personal, as well as national pride, and coveted awards were given each year for the best-looking lengths.

Years of regular scything gave cuttings and embankments a manicured look. A century of such treatment created a high-quality grassland, rich in a variety of wild flowers. Constant cutting or grazing by animals favours one type of plant above all others – the grasses. These form one of the largest plant families, containing some 10 000 species worldwide. Despite their apparently simple straight leaf structure, grasses are highly evolved. They cannot tolerate dense shade, but can survive in areas of low rainfall, and on well-drained slopes, where they are seasonally scorched dry by the sun. Growing on open ground, where there is always likely to be a breeze, grasses can rely on wind pollination. So instead of conspicuous coloured petals to attract insects, the grasses have tiny scales. These grow in clusters, carried high above the surrounding leaves on tall stems, and shed pollen to the wind. The secret of the grasses' ability to endure continual cropping and even flames that destroy all the seeds and leaves, lies partly in the hardy root stock, which is seldom damaged. In addition, the spread of grasses does not rely only on seeds. They send out horizontal stems that creep across the ground, producing new roots and leaves from each joint. The structure of their leaves also contributes to the grasses' success. The leaves of most other plants develop a branched network of veins which carry the sap. The growth of the leaf stops when it reaches full size, and any repair to a cut or torn leaf is limited to

The Oxford ragwort, a native of Sicily (*below*), spread along the lines of the Great Western Railway in the last century. The purple toadflax (*inset*) is another former garden plant now growing wild. *Opposite* Only deep-rooted plants like dandelions (*far right*) survive in the well-drained rail bed, but the banks support many more plants.

preventing leakage of the sap. Grass has its growing point at the base and its veins run in straight rows up the leaf. The leaf grows from the bottom up throughout the life of the plant. So if the upper part is cut or burnt away, the leaf will continue to grow and carpet the railway banks.

When the railways were nationalised in 1948, British Rail took over some 30 000 kilometres of track. By this time, more and more freight was being moved by road, and the railways were gradually declining, with some lines becoming disused. Massive closures of unprofitable branch lines were made between 1962 and 1967, particularly after Dr Beeching's 1963 report, cutting routes down to 18 000 kilometres.

Today the remaining embankments and cuttings that lie either side of the lines cover some 30 000 hectares of land, an area of countryside about half the size of Dartmoor National Park. Yet remarkably, this land contains nearly two-thirds of our native wild plants, more than 2000 species having been recorded. It is only in the last few years that the value of the railway system to wildlife has been fully realised. Wild flowers still grow in great profusion up and down the banks. Primroses flourish and orchids raise their spectacular spikes of flowers. Swathes of ox-eye daisies add a splash of colour to the tangle of grass and pink rosebay willowherb. This invades newly cleared ground, and is among the most successful of all the plants that are found along rail routes.

The flora of rail land is far richer than that of motorways, a fact which owes much to timing. The railways were built before the widespread use of chemical herbicides, which has severely depleted the variety of farmland flowers. Beyond the lethal droplets of chemical killers and spray drift residue, the railways form a last refuge for many species that once germinated and grew in the surrounding fields and hedgerows.

The extent and richness of the railway habitat did not decrease along with the train services. In fact, British Rail's loss was the countryside's gain. All over Britain, wherever you live, there are disused lines nearby, some of which have been turned into nature trails. When a line is abandoned, the track side and cinder beds are soon colonised by the seeds of the annuals growing on adjacent banks. Annuals are vigorous plants capable of growing to full height and flowering in the same season. Species which thrive on well-drained ground, such as thale cress, sticky groundsel, corn salad and whitlow grass, grow first along the track.

Following the annuals come the biennial plants, which generally flower in their second year. Then the first trees and shrubs arrive. Blackthorn forms a thick, almost impenetrable cover, but lets through enough light to allow some bluebells and a little dog's mercury to begin to spread along the ground of the newly formed wood. Elsewhere, the tipping of spent ballast away from the track creates an island shingle bank where long-culmed false oat-grass pushes its way up into the light.

Being ribbon-like, a line may span different types of rock, and this will be reflected in the differing plants that grow along its length. The steep slopes of raised embankments tend to be well drained, while cuttings and drainage ditches are likely to remain wet for much of the year and may contain pools of water. Even in damp footings, where the ballast forms only a thin mulching layer, tall herbs – meadowsweet and nettles – can grow. Further variety has been added by the widespread use of limestone ballast in the past. This has enabled lime-loving plants to grow in areas which would otherwise have been too acid. Stone-built bridges, tunnel mouths and even the station platforms and buildings can provide interesting additions to the local flora where rock outcrops are rare. However, with the demise of a railway line, its supporting structure gives way to new roads or is left to crumble away.

Rail lines are often inaccessible, being sited far from any roads. Many lines which were abandoned a quarter of a century ago are now forgotten, lost in a rising tide of vegetation. Some stretches have been cleared by local authorities to provide amenity walks, cycle routes and, sometimes, nature reserves. Others, such as the picturesque line running along the Dart valley in south Devon, have been given a new lease of life by being sold to private companies. This branch line was originally opened on 1 May 1872 and ran between Totnes and Ashburton, via Buckfastleigh. At first, it was owned by a local railway company, but soon came under the influence and control of the all-powerful Great Western Railway.

The route along the Dart valley was typical of many Great Western branches. Operated by small tank engines and one- or two-coach trains shuttling back and forth, it carried passengers and freight to and from country towns. Pulling out of the busy mainline station of Totnes, the line crossed the river before gently weaving its way upstream. Ambling along the banks of the Dart, it followed the long curves of a steep wooded hillside. After passing under a bridge and pausing at the road gates, the train briefly stopped at the tiny platform of Staverton village station. From there, the railway steamed across a leat bridge with a view over the weir. It went along embankments above surrounding farmland and through cuttings and clearings, before crossing the river once more and pulling into Buckfastleigh station. Then the train moved on to Ashburton, where the south Devon railway terminated. Here the engine was uncoupled and moved back past the carriages, to perform the return journey facing in reverse. Railway turntables,

The dipper (*below*) is typically a bird of clear, fast-flowing water, and walks on the stream bed against the current, searching for its insect prey. *Opposite* Railway bridges crossing such streams are favourite locations for dippers to build their nest. The supporting piers provide a useful perch.

designed to keep engines pulling forwards, were confined to major terminals.

After all the upheaval and earth movement, hammering and clanking, the completion of the railway gave way to the peace of country life, shattered at regular intervals by the passing of a steam train. The embankments and cuttings, bare at first, were soon covered by a new green sward of growth. For twenty years the broad-gauge line ran successfully and, like all the railway services in Britain, was renowned for running on time. It was said that you could set your watch by the train's arrival and departure times. Wild animals quickly became accustomed to such patterns of use and began to inhabit the rail sides. The importance of regular traffic times for wildlife is shown today by the annual increase in badgers killed on the roads during the night after the resetting of clocks at the beginning and end of British Summer Time.

Unlike roads, a railway line is generally only built once, and the major disturbance of its construction fades with the passing of a few seasons. However, the peace of the Dart valley was shattered after two decades by a decision to convert all of the country's broad-gauge track to a standard width. Following months of planning and preparation the sections of line west of Exeter were all changed in one weekend, 20–23 May 1892. Thousands of men working in gangs each tackled an allotted section in an operation even more massive than the line's original construction.

The introduction of paid holidays in the years following the Second World War was responsible for some of the heaviest traffic ever carried on the south Devon railways. However, this boom was shortlived as the age of steam gave way to petrol-driven cars and an expansion of the roads. Passenger rail services were withdrawn from the branch in November 1958. When the axe eventually fell on the line on 10 September 1962, it seemed like the passing of an era. Then the line from Totnes to Buckfastleigh was bought by a private concern to be run as a steam railway. Although the Ashburton connection disappeared beneath the advance of a new A38 dual carriageway, part of the line was saved, along with its wildlife. Perhaps appropriately, the new Dart valley railway was opened by the architect of its original closure, Dr Beeching. Today a regular summer service plies the line, attracting passengers more interested in a steam ride and beautiful country views than simply travelling. The ribbon of railway land is maintained using traditional methods, and this is of great benefit to the wildlife.

Until 1938 railside banks all over Britain were maintained by cutting and burning. Then faster and less labour-intensive spray trains were introduced, dispensing a weed-killing chemical up to three metres from the edge of the track. Plants like the creeping cinquefoil, which sent runners out from the bank to

Overleaf A fox cub at play.

spread over the ballast, were killed to their roots. A whole host of wild plants that had colonised the dry conditions of the line were decimated. Even the Oxford ragwort, which had spread so prolifically across the country, became rarer once again. Chemical spraying has significantly reduced the number of wild plants over recent years and changed the nature of the lines. Today, rosettes of spring whitlow grass thrive because this plant blossoms in April and sets seed before the spray train arrives. Other species, like the small toadflax, grow and flower after spraying, late in the year. The stony surface on which the rails run can become hot and incredibly dry in summer. Only deep tap-rooted plants, like the field horsetail and the toadflax, and fleshy leaved plants, such as the stonecrops, can survive the arid conditions.

The need to keep the track bed free of weeds is undeniable but the spraying of banksides seems totally unnecessary. Increasing pressure from the Nature Conservancy Council may limit the extent of weed control and restore the variety of railside flora. In the meantime, some privately run railways, such as the Dart valley line, are showing what careful and restrained trackside maintenance can achieve. When the Dart line is reopened after its winter rest, yellow splashes of primroses carpet the sides of cuttings. Enthusiasts and workers form small gangs of latter-day lengthmen, clearing weeds from the tracks and removing any fallen branches and dead leaves. The rusted rails soon shine as the steam service begins to run once again.

A train caused the death of one of the railway's first passengers, a dignitary at the opening of Stephenson's railway. The only warnings of an approaching train may be a far-off whistle and a glimpse of rising smoke. A train can move remarkably quietly on level stretches and can cover the ground in a surprisingly short time. For these reasons, access to railway lines has always been restricted and notices warning us of the dangers are placed at all crossing points. Wildlife is not so limited and, with people virtually excluded, the railways provide a haven for creatures which might be persecuted on the surrounding land.

Dry, well-drained banks covered with grass are very attractive to rabbits. Where their numbers are high they may help to give the track sides the appearance of a close-cut lawn. However, holes and scrapes with scattered soil are the main signs of rabbit activity. Their disturbance of the soil encourages annual flowers while the continual close cropping favours dwarf forms of plants. In this way, rabbits can produce a distinctive flora in the area where they live.

Rabbits feed mainly at dawn, dusk and during the night. Their feeding grounds are linked to their holes by a series of runs. Despite a marked dislike for getting their belly fur wet in long grass, they will venture out on the wettest of

nights, keeping the fur dry by shaking their bodies. In areas where they are totally undisturbed, they may emerge during the day. Usually they remain beneath ground by day but continue to feed in a way that is unique to rabbits and the larger hares. Plant material is difficult to digest, and in order to extract the most from each leaf the rabbit uses a process known as refection. It passes very soft faecal pellets and eats them as they are produced so that food travels twice through its gut.

Rabbits are social animals living in large communities divided into groups. A dominant buck defends and rules each group while other members hold a place within a strict hierarchy. All year round, the life of a rabbit centres on a network of burrows, the warren, which forms the basis of its underground home. Only dominant females occupy the main warren. Lower-ranking bucks and does are relegated to blind tunnels, known as stops, or even to less suitable hard ground away from the warren. However, all are linked by a communal alarm system. Any rabbit can alert the entire colony to danger by standing erect or thumping the ground with its hind feet. The force of the thump produces a surprisingly loud sound that seems to resonate in the hollow ground of the rabbit warren.

The territorial drive is strongest in the breeding season beginning in January and extending into August. Young rabbits are born in the main warren or in stops. The nest of grass or moss lined with belly fur is prepared by the doe up to a week before the birth. A litter usually contains three to seven young, which enter the world naked and blind but develop rapidly. Their eyes open after about seven days, by the eighteenth day they have usually emerged from the burrow for the first time, and they are weaned by the age of three weeks. A few days later the stop is deserted and the doe will not use it again that year, choosing a different site for her next litter. Most does produce up to eleven offspring each season and, with young females capable of breeding from three and a half months of age, the rabbit more than lives up to its reputation for fecundity.

The rabbit is not native to Britain, and was introduced by the Normans in the late twelfth century. At first it was kept strictly in captivity, being far too highly valued for its fur and meat to be let loose. Inevitably some escaped and their numbers increased rapidly. Eventually the wild populations started to cause extensive damage to crops and farmland, despite the attention of native predators. Adult rabbits are preyed upon only by foxes and stoats while badgers, buzzards, weasels and domestic cats concentrate on the young.

The greatest threat to the rabbit, however, came from a much smaller animal, the rabbit flea. From 1953 the deadly virus myxomatosis, transmitted by the flea, decimated rabbit populations in a matter of months. It is an ugly disease, and some individuals in the final stages could be seen, blind and deafened from swollen eyes and ears, pathetically attempting to feed on open ground in broad daylight. The depredation of the virus has since declined and today the disease, though widespread, only occurs sporadically. In the areas where it does break out it still claims up to ninety-five per cent of the rabbit population. At first there are easy pickings for predators but as the prey declines so too do they. None relies solely on rabbits for food, and so the predators have managed to survive, although not in such great numbers.

Rabbits can move surprisingly quickly but to see a fox chase and catch one is to appreciate this predator's turn of speed as well. The fox is an opportunist hunter and for most of the year occurs wherever there is sufficient cover to lie up during the day. While breeding during the spring the vixen prefers a more secure resting place. She may take over an abandoned badger set which requires little or no extra digging or, more often, enlarge a rabbit hole in a railway cutting. The vixen digs in a couple of metres before excavating a chamber big enough for her to turn around in. She does not attempt to collect any bedding, but may use a few leaves or grass inherited from the original occupants. Inside the chamber the vixen gives birth to a litter of four or five young which are blind and covered with dark, almost chocolate-brown fur. For the first few weeks she remains in attendance during the day and for much of the night, and continues to suckle her young for six weeks. There is some evidence to suggest that the male brings the vixen food in the first few days after she has given birth. The fox's wary and suspicious nature is well known and at the slightest disturbance by people or dogs, the vixen will move her cubs to another earth. As the young grow she lies up nearby during daylight hours, and the older the cubs get the more adventurous they become.

The sun on a calm May morning made my wait for the appearance of the cubs pleasant if a little warm. They had been spotted the morning before, tumbling down the opposite railway bank onto the line and then disappearing into a bramble patch. A gentle breeze began to blow in my face, which was fortunate as foxes have an acute sense of smell. Then a pair of pointed ears and a small white-tipped tail gave away a cub peering from behind a grass tuft. It tottered up onto a mound and before long another cub came bounding up to begin a play fight. This continued down and along the cinder track and back up onto the bank, before they got caught up in some thorns. To my surprise, a rabbit appeared only a few leaps away from the cubs, making its way slowly across the slope. It stopped occasionally and stood up to peer at the romping cubs, apparently quite used to such antics. Eventually the rabbit disappeared beneath a dense growth of gorse. For more than an hour the fox cubs wandered and explored, and even sat

Below A vixen will enlarge an old rabbit burrow in which to give birth to her young. Fox cubs are born with a thick coat of black fur which turns chocolate and then red-brown over the next eight weeks until they are weaned. *Opposite* Young rabbits are almost naked at birth, but within three weeks they are able to leave the burrow to feed on clover.

watching as a train clattered past, before finally returning to their earth deep underground.

Further along the track, the railway converges on running water and a strong, erosion-resistant construction is needed to ensure that the line is safe. A series of sluice gates controls a mill leat which diverts water away from the main river and under the railway. The bridge, hardly noticeable from the line, is a flat iron structure with large girders supporting tonnes of stone ballast and steel track. The fast-flowing water divides around two central piers of stone which give additional support to the diagonal span. A ledge just above the water line was a design feature of supporting piers, and has proved an ideal place for the dipper to rest before swimming in search of food. The dipper, a small white-breasted bird of fast-flowing streams, has adapted to a life alongside as well as under the water. It gained its name from its habit of continually bobbing up and down. With wings partly outstretched and angled to keep itself down, the dipper walks on the bed of the stream against the flow of the water, feeding mainly on aquatic insect larvae.

As well as being a vantage point from which to feed, the bridge also provides the dipper with a place to breed. In the dark shadows under the iron structure, where a girder meets the stone wall, a pair have built a nest overhanging the water. The soft mound of moss is lined with grass and dead leaves, and has an entrance pointing down towards the stream. The female alone incubates the eggs, which usually number five. Her vigil may last for eighteen days and during this time she is fed by her mate. About three weeks after hatching, the young dippers leave the nest and are so well adapted to their aquatic life that they can dive and swim even before they can fly. Once the first brood has flown, the parents nest again, and may do so three times in one season.

As I sat concealed not far from the dippers' nest, the sound of running water echoed beneath the walls of the bridge and the outside world appeared bright viewed from the shadows. By now the birds were flying up to the nest frequently, bringing beakfuls of larval insects to their brood of hungry chicks. The rumbling sound of an approaching train grew in only a few seconds to a deafening roar. The adult birds flew away when the train reached the bridge and the rhythmic clatter of wheels thundered overhead. The din receded as quickly as it had arrived, and the natural sounds of running water and distant birdsong arose again. When the parent birds returned, the smell of smoke still lingered in the air.

Summer brings a riot of colour to the line as a succession of plants raise their heads and slowly set seed. Not all the flowers are of native origin. The tall yellow blooms of goldenrod are garden escapes, perhaps self-sown from the overflowing tubs and flower beds that still adorn the little station of Staverton. Here on a warm and sultry summer evening I watched the last train of the day pull away with loud chuffs of smoke and venting of steam. The signals were set and the time of tomorrow's first train shown on the dial of a board. The stationmaster, with a black jacket thrown over his arm, locked up and made his way home, leaving a station yard far from devoid of life. The stacks of timber and rusting remains of rail ironwork were overgrown with a miniature jungle of tangled roots, matted grass and a forest of stems and leaves. Grasshoppers and crickets kept up an incessant song while a soft high-pitched twittering, coming from the dry grass, gave away the presence of a hunting shrew.

The common shrew is a tiny, fast-moving mammal that at a fleeting glance may look like a very small mouse. However, the shrew is unrelated to the gnawing, chisel-toothed, mainly vegetarian rodents, and any resemblance is purely superficial. The carnivorous shrew has a long sensitive nose and sharp little teeth to help it forage for insects and worms, and it will not hesitate to tackle surprisingly big prey. It lives and feeds at ground level, where it makes tunnels and runs both on and just under the surface.

Shrews are incredibly busy creatures, hunting both day and night with bouts of activity interspersed by short periods of rest. The search for food consumes most of their active life, for shrews must eat their own body weight each day just to survive. Their maximum life span is only two years and few shrews reach old age. Older individuals are particularly vulnerable when they are ousted from the best cover by the strongly territorial young shrews. There are, however, only a few predators that will touch them. The domestic cat kills many, but apparently finds shrews distasteful and seldom eats them. Owls are not so discerning, and will take large numbers of shrews, swallowing them whole.

In the last glow of dusk, a barn owl was hunting in slow buoyant flight along the railway grassland. It hovered briefly on shimmering white wings before plunging to the ground. When it emerged, it was clutching not a shrew but the principal prey of predatory birds, a field vole. Larger than the shrew, the field vole is a small blunt-nosed mammal with small ears and eyes and a very short tail. It often occurs in considerable numbers in old pasture and on railway banks, where it creates a series of runs linking nests in grass tussocks or under discarded sheets of corrugated iron to feeding grounds of tender young shoots and leaves. In this way, the vole can remain hidden for much of the time and is only exposed to aerial attack when it explores new ground or crosses open areas, such as roads or railway tracks.

Voles feed at any time, though their activity peaks at dawn and dusk. The

Opposite Barn owls prey mainly on voles and mice and, for that reason, favour permanent grasslands with well established hedgerows for hunting. *Below* The female glow-worm is flightless and climbs grass stems to signal for a mate. Even the eggs (*bottom*) emit a slight glow and are laid on grass-covered soil.

long-tailed field or wood mouse, on the other hand, is strictly nocturnal. During the day the wood mouse stays below ground in a labyrinth of tiny tunnels. There it may consume a food store of nuts and seeds in comparative safety. The small and sinuous weasel can explore to such depths, as can the venomous adder, but the wood mouse nearly always has more than one exit from its nest.

When the sun sets, the wood mice come to the surface, where their large ears and eyes help to guide them through the dark undergrowth. They forage over large distances, often covering several hundred metres or more. During summer days, the passing trains draw many plant seeds along the track, and these fall between the stone ballast. Under the cover of night, wood mice scuttle along the line in search of this food. Though they are mainly seed and fruit eaters, wood mice will also eat any snails and insects they find.

As the last glimmer of light still lingers above the steep banks of the railway cutting, tiny lights can be seen glowing in the dark. These are emitted by one of the strangest yet most enchanting of all the creatures of the night, the glow-worm. Despite its common name, this insect is actually a beetle. The glow-worm produces light at all stages of its life from egg to adult, but only the female is brightly luminous. She probably gave rise to its name for, being wingless with a distinctly segmented body, the female bears some resemblance to a worm. The male, however, is winged and flies in search of a mate.

The glow-worm's light is created by a complex chemical reaction involving luciferin and the enzyme luciferase in the presence of oxygen and water. Another substance, usually known by its abbreviation, ATP, acts as an energiser. The process is extraordinarily efficient with nearly ninety per cent of the chemical energy being converted into light. (In contrast, a tungsten filament bulb converts only 5.5 per cent of the energy it consumes into light.) The quality of the glow-worm's light is also remarkable for it falls almost entirely within the yellow–green band of the spectrum. The light contains practically no heat or infra-red, no ultra-violet and no other colours, and so appears to us as a cool green glow.

The female glow-worm climbs onto a prominent leaf, a plant stem or even a stone on the track, to begin her display. The greenish glow comes from the last three abdominal segments, just under her tail. She curls the tail round, points it skywards and twists it slowly, first to one side then to the other, signalling into the night.

The male emits only a feeble light, but has far more sensitive vision than his mate. Flying close to the ground, he homes in on the female's brightly lit beacon. When mating takes place, they turn off their lights.

The larval offspring are miniature versions of the female but carry a weaker light. Unlike the adults, which are not known to eat, the larvae hunt for slowly moving prey, particularly snails. It is for this reason that glow-worms are confined almost exclusively to chalk and limestone areas of England, where snails abound in damp hedgerows and meadows. The larva follows the slime trail of a snail, nose to the ground. When the larva catches a snail, it uses its tubular jaws to inject a dark fluid, which first paralyses the snail and then reduces it to liquid. The resultant soup is sucked up by the young glow-worm.

These extraordinary creatures are not as common as they used to be, and there are several possible reasons for their decline. Both adults and young fall prey to hedgehogs and toads, and, to a lesser extent, frogs and spiders. However, the most marked decline has been in areas of urban development, on drained land and where there is increasing use of insecticides. Even more insidious may be the effect of light pollution. As long ago as 1791, the naturalist Gilbert White noted that 'male glow-worms, attracted by the light of the candles, come into the parlour'. The increasing urban sprawl and bright road lighting could be luring male glow-worms away from the females' beacons. Only in places far from artificial illuminations do the female glow-worms stand a chance of being found, for example in a dark and remote railway cutting.

On a still summer's night a closed train station can still attract some visitors. The howling screams of two warring tom cats were rudely terminated by a dustbin crashing to the ground. A fox, drawn by the scent of discarded food, had managed to dislodge the lid and overturn the container. After rummaging among the remains of passengers' packed lunches, it picked up and proudly removed some chicken bones. With the returning light came the songs of birds, including a thrush on a nearby tree, a robin on a wall and, highest of all, a blackbird on the apex of the engine shed roof.

A large train standing for any length of time can gain some unexpected passengers. One pair of blackbirds had built their nest behind a large bowl-shaped bell that fitted between two carriages. Sheltered by the shed and hidden from sight, it formed a safe elevated platform on which to rear the young. While the blackbirds travelled first class, one pair of swallows went freight, taking up residence in a wagon. They swooped in through the open sliding door to feed their brood of young. Another pair of swallows had built their nest high up in the maintenance shed, above all the metallic noise and welding sparks, bodies and bogies of engines being rebuilt and repaired. The swallow makes its nest from a mixture of mud, grass and other plant materials. The availability of mud and a ready supply of insects are the main reason why swallows tend to nest near a

Some birds frequently nest close to man. *Below left* The robin nests in a shed while this blackbird (*below right*) has taken up a first-class residence on some carriages left in the sidings. *Opposite* The warm, dry conditions of railway ballast and the banks in cuttings are ideally suited to the slow worm – a harmless, legless lizard.

source of water. When the engines take on water from the trackside tank, the overhead pipe spills water along the line. Swallows take mud from these temporary pools, while noisy flocks of the ever-present house sparrows fly in for a drink and a bathe.

Far from the station, where the railway cuts through a wood or across wet ground, its raised banks have become a highway for roe deer. In the twilight, they emerge from cover and make their way, either singly or in small female and fawn groups, to their nocturnal feeding grounds in the fields. Returning by the railway track at dawn, they melt back into the woods.

Another regular traveller along the line is the badger. Seen from behind, its dense coat swayed as it ambled along. Such a loose skin is essential for an animal that spends so much of its time beneath ground, squeezing through tunnels and between tree roots. As I watched in the half light, the badger stopped frequently to listen and scent the air before investigating and pawing at the ground, perhaps searching for a beetle. Badgers consume large numbers of these ground-dwelling insects, as can be seen from the number of hard beetle remains in their droppings. The badger then continued down the embankment following one of its well-beaten paths. The badger's trail may have been made soon after the railway's completion, or it may be centuries old, used by generations of badgers. All the badgers living within a sett have a common group smell, which can be recognised by others. Where the trails run near the edge of their territory, strategically placed latrine pits act as a calling card to neighbouring badgers. In this way groups can mark and hold the large territories in which they forage.

As well as journeying along railway lines, badgers also travel underground. They are powerful animals, capable of digging in surprisingly hard ground, but the earth must be well drained, such as that of railway banks. Huge mounds of excavated earth spilling down the slope are generally the first signs that badgers are digging a sett. If a hard core of large rocks is uncovered, the badger may give up, but otherwise it will keep digging. Typically, a sett is between ten and twenty metres long but it can extend for up to 100 metres in a labyrinth of tunnels and chambers. Such considerable feats of animal engineering undermine the railway and pose a particularly serious threat where mainline intercity trains pass at high speed. Then the badgers have to be removed, sometimes with mechanical excavators and expert help, and taken to a new home. Fortunately, the diggings seldom become extensive, and badgers generally prefer the shelter of nearby wooded slopes to the exposed sides of a railway line.

Where trackside trees are regularly trimmed, species such as hazel send out vigorous, dense new growth. In season this yields a fine crop of hazel nuts, which many animals feast upon. The nuts on the ends of the thinnest branches, out beyond even the grey squirrel's reach, are collected by dormice. Though rare in many counties, there are some thriving colonies of dormice in Devon. These attractive, agile mice, characterised by a long bushy tail, are almost entirely nocturnal. In order to see their arboreal antics, I sat quietly in a suitable wood at the onset of dusk, facing west. Against the afterglow of the sun, I glimpsed their tiny shapes as they leapt around high up in the hazel branches. In midsummer, the dormice have only a few hours to forage before the sun rises again.

An hour or two after sunrise, the warmth had brought lizards and slow-worms out to bask in its rays. During the cool of night these reptiles are inactive, but as the air temperature rises so too does that of their blood. By flattening their bodies they expose a larger surface area to the sun and are soon warm enough to begin to hunt. Despite their name and lack of legs, slow-worms are close relatives of lizards and eat similar foods, such as insects, spiders and worms. While lizards will take almost anything they can swallow, slow-worms seem to prefer slugs and small snails.

Usually keeping well hidden, the slow-worm is far more common than is generally realised. Dry sunny slopes are particularly favoured by the slow-worm and recently some have even reached as far as the centre of London, along railway banks. They are well suited to movement below ground and under surface vegetation, where legs would be more of a hindrance than a help in the tangle of stems and roots. They make tunnels in soft earth and leaf litter and often lie with just their heads above the surface, reducing the chance of being spotted by a predator.

Slow-worms curl up under discarded sheets of metal, especially corrugated iron, and beneath stones and pieces of wood. Despite an apparent lack of interest in taking adult ants, they are also regularly found lying in ants' nests, surrounded by the insect hordes. This may be purely coincidental, as ants too often occur under flat stones. Slow-worms are not the speediest of Britain's five native reptiles, but when warm they can move fairly fast. Despite this, mortality is high. Adults are regularly killed by birds of prey, most carnivorous mammals and even domestic poultry. Most birds consider the young to be worms, and will eat them if uncovered.

Female slow-worms give birth in late summer to what often appear to be fully formed young. In fact, the slow-worm lays eggs but the egg membrane ruptures at birth or very soon after. In a cold, wet year a pregnant female may not give birth. Instead she hibernates and produces her young in the following spring. For this reason, small slow-worms may be found throughout the summer months. In

Opposite The caterpillars of peacock, small tortoiseshell and red admiral butterflies feed on nettles and the adults survive on nectar sipped from railside flowers – particularly the buddleia, which is often found in railyards. *Below* Shaggy inkcaps grow in the damp beneath the steam engine water supply.

contrast to the adults, the young are often found in damp ground, only moving to drier areas after a few months' growth. This may reflect a change in their diet or simply in the size of their prey.

In August, the platform of Buckfastleigh station is filled with a milling throng of passengers eagerly awaiting the arrival of the steam train. Even in the heyday of steam, the station would not have been so full of people. Amid much hissing and the excited cries of the crowd, the train came to a standstill and the engine was shunted back to the other end. Then doors slammed, a whistle blew, and the train departed once more in clouds of steam and acrid smoke.

Beyond the platform, in the shelter afforded by the buildings, a brightly lit corner was warmed by the sun. Tortoiseshell butterflies basked on the rails and along the cinder track, resting between feeds. The adult's diet consists almost entirely of nectar, a sweet-tasting fluid rich in energy. It is produced by insect-pollinated flowers with some providing far more than others. Among the best at this time of the year are the flamboyant trailing blooms of the common buddleia. We tend to take this plant for granted, because it grows on waste land and spreads all too easily in the garden. Even when cut back close to the ground, its long stems can grow over head height by the end of the summer season. Buddleia's spectacular spikes are composed of hundreds of flowers coloured lilac, lavender or even deep purple. It is a native of China and was introduced to this country relatively recently, so few creatures have developed a taste for its long leaves, except sometimes the caterpillar of the mullein moth. Buddleia's nectar, however, is produced in copious quantities, and is much sought after by insects. As the nectar lies at the base of the flower tube, only those insects with a long proboscis can reach it, such as butterflies and moths. In late summer, tortoiseshells, peacock butterflies, red admirals and painted ladies cover the buddleia, giving it its other name, the butterfly bush.

The buddleia will continue to produce flowers into early October but by then many of its bright-winged visitors will have departed. Some will have died in the increasingly cold nights. Others, like the tortoiseshell, will have sought out the shelter of an engine shed, ticket office, open carriage or goods wagon in which to pass the winter deep in hibernation.

At the close of summer, the regular daily service running on the Dart valley line ends. In September the engines and carriages stand silently in the sidings and under the shelter of a lofty shed. Most of the flowers that have managed to survive along the tracks or in the cinder-strewn ground of the station have already set seed. In places where the track bed is not well drained, the spore-bearing bodies of fungi have pushed aside the ballast stones and force their way up into the path of a breeze. Shaggy inkcaps, which are common fungi of meadows and grass banks, grow outside the signal box, releasing millions of tiny spores to the wind.

As the autumn leaves turn golden brown, the rail surfaces begin to lose their metallic shine. Without the regular wear of wheels, the inevitable layer of rust slowly forms. A buzzard now uses one of the unused signals as a regular vantage point to watch for small mammals along the line. On autumn days there is little warmth to create thermals, the rising columns of air on which these birds ride. So the buzzard conserves energy by sitting and waiting for prey to make a false move. Kestrels, too, spend much of their time hunting in this static way, only resorting to an energy-consuming hover while searching open ground. The rank vegetation that grew so high during the spring and summer now begins to die down. Its decaying leaves and stems fall back to the ground. They not only return vital nutrients to the soil, but also create a tangled layer beneath which plants and animals can survive the winter. Butterfly pupae, insect larvae and even glow-worms, can lie protected until the warmth of a new season allows them to emerge again.

The lines of Britain's extensive railway network provide a unique habitat for wildlife. Some pass through areas of outstanding natural beauty, along cliffs and dramatic sea coasts, or wind their way up hills and over moorland. Others ply city routes lined with tall buildings of concrete and brick. However, all share one feature in common, and that is the nature of the line.

The Dart valley railway spans time as well as distance. Steam railways are a direct link with the past, preserving not only engines, rolling stock, signals and stations, but also the animals and plants which thrive along their banks. While the surrounding countryside has changed dramatically over the last century, a vestige of its flowering variety can still be seen along the verges as the trains whistle by. If the closure of the Dart valley railway in winter is an annual replay of the axing of so many branch lines in the past, then its reopening in the spring echoes the coming of an age of steam and its wildlife.

CHAPTER 4

The Quarry

High on the north-facing slopes of Dartmoor, granite tors are shrouded by low cloud and the steep walls of a cliff are partly hidden by swirling mist. The sound of people and machinery seems alien in such bleak and forbidding surroundings, yet people have worked up here for centuries, hewing rock from the ground. Since the Stone Age, pits have been dug across Britain to obtain flints and other stone. The Romans built cities with the aid of master masons, and through the Middle Ages people excavated blocks for building and slates for roofs. This ancient quarrying has transformed pockets of land scattered across the country, from the flint mines of Grimes Graves in East Anglia and the medieval limestone quarries in the Barnock Hills of Cambridgeshire to the hand-drilled and split rocks which can still be seen on Dartmoor.

Today, Meldon quarry on Dartmoor is a main source of the hard rock used as ballast by British Rail. As I looked over the edge of this vast pit, the workers at the base were dwarfed by the enormous vehicles standing nearby and these, in turn, appeared tiny in such a huge space. A series of giant steps had been carved out of the moor, rising from the floor of the quarry up to just below the skyline. A siren sounded and echoed back from the hills, to be repeated a few minutes later.

This brought the noise and movement of work to a halt and only the high-pitched calls of wheeling jackdaws could be heard. Many more were perched on the cliffs and ledges that surround the main pit, seeming alert and expectant. As the wail of the last siren faded, a bell began to toll, ringing and resounding around the bare rock. At this, the jackdaws took to the air and flew quickly away from the cliffs. Some alighted on the tall machinery that pounds rock into smaller stones, while the rest remained aloft, circling in a flock.

The blast, though expected, still came as a shock as seven tonnes of high explosive moved more than 35 000 tonnes of rock. The detonation was over in less than a second and felt like a single event. In reality, it was a carefully planned and controlled series of explosions along a line of drilled holes. The effect of the blast was soon hidden by a vast rolling cloud of dust as the solid cliff crumpled into rock rubble. Some boulders were blown into the sky but few rose far before tumbling back to the ground.

Even before the dust had settled, the all-clear siren sounded and the jackdaws returned to the ledges of the adjacent cliffs. For over 100 years this quarry has been worked for its granite, and for the past few decades the same series of warnings has heralded a blast. Jackdaws, like all members of the crow family, are intelligent birds, and have learnt to associate the sirens and bell with an imminent explosion. They depart on cue, only returning after the all-clear has sounded in case there is a second blast.

The fact that wildlife can tolerate the continual upheaval of a working quarry seems remarkable. Yet nature is extraordinarily tenacious, often surviving against what appear to be overwhelming odds. Throughout the thousands of millions of years that plants have been evolving, life has kept pace with the sometimes cataclysmic geological and climatic changes and colonised any new environments created. The creatures which dwell on cliffs must adapt quickly, for they are among the most precarious and unstable of habitats. Coastal cliffs are formed by ocean winds driving waves against the land to pound and shatter the rock face. Inland, such features are not so common. Upheaval of the crust may tear apart sections of the Earth and create precipices along faults in the rock. Over longer periods of time, the weather can also transform the land. Rain pouring over the surface is driven deep into crevices by the wind, permeating the finest cracks. When the temperature falls below freezing, the water turns to ice and expands. In areas which are warm by day and frozen at night, the water continually contracts and expands until eventually the rock fractures and entire sections fall away. So enormous are the destructive forces of the weather that over vast periods of time entire mountains are eroded away. Ice is the chief agent of mechanical erosion, but the shattering of rock exposes a greater surface area to more subtle wear as water reacts with other substances to form acid or alkaline solutions which slowly dissolve away the rock.

The exposed granite tors of Dartmoor are the only visible remains of a mountain range formed from molten rock which issued from the Earth's core. It solidified to a hard igneous rock that weathers slowly and so still forms the impressive slabs and boulder piles that today stand proud on each hill. Sculpted by the elements over thousands of years, any sharp edges have long since been worn and rounded. Every exposed surface is etched and pitted, giving the granite its familiar rugged look. Only in the recent past, where people have split the rock using explosive force, have smooth clean lines and jagged edges intruded upon the land. When a quarry reaches the end of its working life, it is abandoned, leaving huge tips of spoil piled high and a massive scar laid bare.

Within a few seasons of a quarry's closure, a pair of ravens may set up home. These large birds of the open moors will nest in trees but frequently choose to breed on an inaccessible ledge, halfway up the steep side of a man-made cliff. They will eat almost anything, from insects and shellfish to harvest-spilt grain and even acorns. Today they are most commonly seen in upland sheep-rearing areas of Britain, where they feed on carrion and afterbirth during the lambing season.

The raven was once a common scavenger, occurring in the centre of cities. In Tudor times, ravens along with kites were valued as cleansers of English streets and were protected in and around towns by Henry VIII. Even today, ravens can be found in the centre of the capital, living in the Tower of London. The reason for this dates back to the reign of Charles II, when an astronomical observatory was built on one of the towers. It soon became a focal point for flocks of ravens, which used it as an elevated perch. The astronomers appealed to the king to have the birds removed. However, an ancient legend was brought to the king's attention, which stated that if the ravens ever left the Tower of London, the White Tower would crumble and the monarchy would come to an end. A royal proclamation was thus made that the Tower should at all times retain several birds. From that day to this, at least six ravens have been kept at the Tower. They are traditionally treated as soldiers, each one given a name, rank and number, and even a wage. Their wages pay for a yeoman ravenmaster and a regular supply of food for the birds themselves.

The ravens resident in the Tower today are direct descendants of birds from Dartmoor. During the dark days of the Second World War, when Hitler's forces were sweeping across Europe, morale in Britain needed to be kept high. Ravens

Opposite The raven is now found only in the north and west of Britain and, apart from coastal cliffs, only disused quarries provide the sheer faces and rocky ledges for the birds to breed. *Below* The jackdaw has even learnt to live in active quarries, taking heed of warning sirens before a blast.

still survived in the Tower, despite the blitz, but their numbers had begun to decline. With the legend in mind, it was decided to introduce new blood, and young ravens collected from several sites on Dartmoor were introduced to the Tower. To this day, they and the monarchy still thrive.

The breeding season of the raven begins early, often well before winter's end. In contrast to their sometimes ponderous, heavy-winged flight as they patrol in pairs or family groups over the moor, their courtship flights can be breathtaking. A pair will tumble high in the sky, half-closing their wings, rolling and turning before climbing once more, and even flying for short distances upside-down. These aerial antics, which may continue for days on end, are a prelude to a mating ceremony on the ground. This performance commences with much bowing and neck-stretching from both male and female, followed by a ruffling of the throat feathers. Then the male spreads his wings and tail while crouching and stretching his neck upwards with the bill pointing downwards. Sometimes he jumps into the air or gently preens the female's face with his bill. Ravens mate for life and this ceremony is repeated every year to help cement the bond. However, ravens soaring on outstretched wings high above a quarry are not necessarily performing part of a courtship display. Like all members of the crow family, they sometimes indulge in exuberant flights and odd behaviour, such as hanging upside-down from a branch, for no apparent reason.

On Dartmoor, where trees are sparse and often stunted, ravens nest on a few suitable natural rock faces or in old quarries. Large sticks form a base on which other twigs and coarse material lie, bound together by a mixture of mud and mosses. The nest is well lined with grass tufts covered with sheep's wool and the hair from cattle or deer. Here, in late winter, the female usually lays four pale blue-green eggs with dark markings. For the next few weeks she incubates the eggs, while her mate brings her food. Through moorland mist and heavy rain, sleet and snow, the female sits tight, keeping the eggs warm and dry. After some twenty days the young will hatch, provided that the nest has remained undisturbed.

The nest is usually sited on a ledge lit only by a morning or evening sun, and sheltered from the prevailing wind. Its inaccessibility keeps the eggs safe from most natural predators, but not, unfortunately, from humans. Each spring steep rock faces attract teams of climbers striving to improve their technique or test new equipment. Unaware of the nest, they can keep the female, and the vital warmth she provides, away from the eggs. High up on the moors daytime temperatures are still low in spring, and it may only take an hour for the unprotected eggs to chill, killing the embryo young within the shell.

In addition, there are people who deliberately kill the chicks before they hatch. In Victorian days the gathering of natural history specimens, such as fossils, shells, butterflies and birds' eggs, was a widely accepted pastime that sometimes added to the store of biological knowledge. Today such individual collections are no longer necessary and can threaten the existence of an already rare species. Despite this, some people wantonly persist in acquiring and owning a huge variety of eggs. They do not take just one egg from a nest, which would be bad enough. Modern collectors are avid and obsessive people who steal entire clutches each year to profit from an illegal trade or simply to line cabinet drawers. Every season many ravens lose one or more clutches to collectors, despite legal protection and the efforts of local bird watchers. Ravens will mate and relay when their eggs are stolen; but they have their limits and will eventually abandon all attempts to breed that year if the nest is robbed again.

Although several more remote raven nests had already been raided this spring, the one I was watching from a safe distance away had remained unmolested and three chicks had hatched within the last few days. The young were blind and helpless at first, and the female stayed with them, keeping them well covered. Usually the male alone feeds the female and young for the first week, announcing his arrival with a characteristic deep guttural croak. However, this female had two adult ravens in attendance, for another female was helping to feed the young. While such behaviour is not unknown among other species of birds, it is rare in ravens. The helper is usually an offspring from the previous year's brood and is, therefore, assisting in the rearing of its own brothers and sisters and gaining valuable experience for when it tends its own young. Birds seldom adopt the role of helper for more than a single breeding season. By the second week the young were stronger and kept warm by a dense dull brown covering of downy feathers. The adult birds now spent an hour or more away from the nest, although one often remained close by, sometimes out of sight of the nest.

During such periods, a pair of jackdaws would seize their chance to sweep down on the nest. They did not harm the young, which were almost as big as the jackdaws themselves. Instead they pulled the sticks and tufts of wool from beneath the chicks to furnish their own home. Jackdaws nest in holes in buildings or cliff walls, and by early spring almost all suitable sites are occupied. This pair had selected a hole behind the ledge on which the ravens had built their untidy pile of twigs. An adult raven would quickly see off any jackdaw that approached the ledge. So the pair waited at a safe distance until the young were alone and then dived down to steal nesting material and enter their hole.

Opposite A granite quarry abandoned in the last century provides shelter from the prevailing moorland winds. Here heathers bloom early and trees can grow. *Below* Old drill holes (*inset*) still show where the rocks were split by hand, and birds like the wheatear (*main picture*) nest amongst the piles of stone.

After five and a half weeks, the raven chicks' downy covering had been outgrown by black plumage and they were fully fledged. No longer confined to the nest, they made their first hesitant flights within the quarry walls, flapping from ledge to ledge. Soon, they only converged on the nest when an adult returned with a scavenged meal. Within two months of hatching, the young ravens were following their parents out over the moor, and the quarry no longer echoed to their calls.

For the first few years after the closure of a quarry, the walls of the ravens' home are bare. This landscape carved by people presents as forbidding a surface as the ground in the aftermath of the last ice age would have done. Now, as then, the first colonisers to begin cloaking the surface are the lichens.

These remarkable plants can thrive on the harsh, sterile surface of newly exposed rock, withstanding the extremes of drought and drenching. They are a successful group of plants and some 16 000 genera are known worldwide, of which 150 are found in Britain alone. Some genera are rare and represented by only a few species, while others, like *Cladonia*, may contain nearly forty species. Lichens may be so thin and lie so close to the surface on which they grow that they can be mistaken for part of the rock. Others, especially those species found on moorland trees, are more conspicuous, festooning branches in a miniature slow-growing cascade.

Lichens are unique in being composed of two separate and quite distinct types of plant, an alga and a fungus. They grow together to their mutual benefit, forming a partnership known as symbiosis. The fungus produces acids which eat into the hard rock, enabling the lichen to cling to the smooth surface. The alga absorbs the rock minerals dissolved by the fungal acid and produces the green pigment chlorophyll. With the help of sunlight and chlorophyll, the alga synthesises the rock minerals, and carbon dioxide and water from the air, into food which sustains both alga and fungus.

In lichens, the symbiosis is of greater benefit to the fungus than the alga. The fungus could not survive alone on bare rock as it would be unable to manufacture its own food. However, protected by the fungus from intense light, and the extremes of drought and soaking, the alga can survive harsher conditions than it could on its own. Their association gives the fungus and alga a leading edge, allowing lichens to colonise areas unoccupied by other plants.

Lichens can live for a very long time but many are slow-growing. Those found encrusting rocks at high altitude are especially slow, as there may be only a few days each year when conditions are right for growth. Some take more than half a century to cover one square centimetre and perhaps thousands of years to grow to dinner-plate size. These pioneers of the plant world are found up to 7000 metres high on mountain tops, and survive even on rocks surrounded by polar ice. However, lichens can only thrive where the air is clean. As a result their presence or absence is a remarkably good indicator of the level of pollutants in the air.

Once the lichens have gained a toehold on the bare slopes, the first few particles of soil soon become lodged. Then wind-blown spores and seeds can settle and the rocks in the deserted quarry, where the sound of blasting still seems to echo in the hills, become tinged with green. In tiny cracks and crevices mosses and ferns begin to grow, watered by the damp moorland air. Close relatives of the mosses, the liverworts, thrive in corners shaded from the sun and soaked by the splashing of a moorland stream. The liverworts spread a thin green thallus, a structure that is neither a stem nor leaf but fulfils the functions of both.

After many years the quarry becomes submerged beneath a rising sea of plant growth as trees become established, and the ground is clothed in a grass sward.

Even in the shelter of a quarry, few trees manage to survive the cold moorland winters, but two are better suited to the harsh conditions. Small wind-stunted hawthorns, with grotesquely distorted limbs, grow in the lee of rocks out on the moor. In the quarries they are not so restricted and grow into fine trees. The other hardy species, the rowan or mountain ash, can be found not only on the quarry base but also on its walls. Rowan seedlings will grow on a ledge, in a crevice or wherever their roots can gain a foothold. In late summer they produce an abundance of bright red berries which are highly attractive to certain birds. In quarries near the moorland edge it is the familiar blackbird which feasts on the fruit. The closely related ring ousel, a summer visitor to the high moor, will also feed on the fruit before flying south. It takes only about twenty minutes for seeds to pass through a bird's gut and be deposited with its droppings, so rowan seeds seldom spread far.

In one old quarry, a hole in a wall is all that remains of the quarry clock, which once marked the hours of the working day. For eighty years, the ravens have reared successive generations and the colony of jackdaws has steadily grown. Piles of rubble, rotting timber, empty windows and doorways show that the structure of the quarry's past life is slowly decaying away. The wood-beamed roofs of the buildings have collapsed and only the shells of the solid stone walls still stand.

Old buildings are used by many mammals and birds, either as a roost or a place in which to rear their young. Stock doves, which also nest in holes in trees and cliffs, have taken readily to disused buildings. Barn owls occupy the larger dwellings, nesting on top of a wall that is still sheltered by a roof or, preferably,

Opposite Damp shady places are ideal conditions for ferns to grow.
Below Stone walls and some hard wood rafters are all that remain of a by-gone industrial age as nature reclaims long-lost ground.

up on the first floor of a two-storey building. The owls will even nest in the floor, secure in the space between the timber joists, if rotten boards provide an access hole. Where owls are absent, bats will inhabit the gaps between the stones of ruins and find hanging space up among the rafters. Of the fifteen types of bat found in Britain, four are mainly woodland species frequenting hollow trees. These are also the rarest of bats and virtually nothing is known of their natural history. In contrast, the rest tend to live in close contact with people and their structures. Up to ninety per cent of them are thought to inhabit buildings for at least part of the year.

The dominant feature of some quarries is not their cliffs, but their spoil heaps. When a quarry is hewn from a hillside, little material needs to be removed before reaching the rock. On level sites, however, large quantities of soil and unsuitable stone, known as overburden, may have to be cleared away. Today, such material is sold or utilised in some way, but in the past it was considered waste and dumped nearby. Over a few decades, the mounds of overburden rose up into man-made mountains forming a steep-sided backdrop to the works.

Once a quarry is abandoned the mounds, like the cliff walls, are colonised by a succession of plants. On large spoil heaps over fifty years old it is not unusual to find more than 100 species of plants, including several different shrubs and trees. The most spectacular colonisers are undoubtedly the orchids, which rank as the second largest family of plants in the world. Although these plants may take several years to grow from seed to flower, they are often pioneers of newly exposed land. Orchids produce millions of minute seeds that can be carried considerable distances by a breeze. To germinate and grow, the seeds must fall in and around the base of fungi, which break down material in the soil enabling the orchids to absorb food. They remain underground for up to four years as leafless shoots before seeing the light of day. Finally, the elegant purple spikes of spotted orchids appear high on the bare scree and boulder-strewn summit of a mountainous heap. There they await the arrival of pollinating insects before they too can shed their seeds to the wind.

Years of waste tipping produce an artificial slope as inviting to some birds as any clitter flowing down from a rocky tor. The attractively marked wheatear is a summer visitor to Britain, occasionally arriving as early as February but more usually in March or the beginning of April. Its conspicuous white rump shows as it flits across the moorland but it is more often seen perched on prominent stones.

Wheatears only live in areas where rabbits or sheep maintain a short turf, on which the birds find their insect food. Some remain around the coast, on cliff-tops and shingle shores, while a few inhabit lowland areas. The majority, however, live in the uplands of Britain, especially where there are scatterings of rocks. They nest beneath boulders, in scree-slopes, or down any suitable hole, including rabbit burrows and holes in walls.

Pied wagtails, with their ever-wagging tail and quick flight, also feed on insects. These striking birds are found all over Britain, but they are largely summer visitors in Scotland, remaining throughout the year in most of England. There is hardly a quarry in the country that has not at some time played host to a pair. In early summer they build a nest in a safe and sheltered place, such as the scattered mounds and mountains of waste. One such scattering of rocks surrounds a quarry that lies in the lee of the famous landmark of Haytor. Early in the last century, the granite from Haytor quarries was cut and transported to London where its inherent strength and quality lent support to many fine works of architecture, including the columns of the British Museum library and the arches of London Bridge. The silence that followed the ending of works in 1837 still pervades the quarry's now flooded depths. Huge slabs linger by a dark pool, alongside the rusting remains of a crane with its giant wooden arm partly submerged.

Water plays an important part in the life and sometimes the death of a quarry. Before the invention of powerful pumps, quarries were under constant threat of flooding. While shallow depressions may fill with rain and dry up again almost as quickly, many deeper pits become filled permanently with water. The moorland soil gradually leaches into these lakes and its acidity renders the water unsuitable for much plant growth. In winter the lakes, often deep and darkened by years of peat-laden seasonal streams, are remarkably clear with an apparent lack of life. However, by summer the bog pondweed is flowering and its floating leaves provide cover for animals, such as the palmate newt.

The palmate is the smallest of Britain's three native newts. In upland areas it may remain in water throughout the year but it emerges in spring from a hibernation beneath nearby rocks and makes its way to the water. Here it feeds on tiny freshwater crustaceans, replenishing its food reserves and rapidly gaining in weight. During the breeding season, the male palmate has a straw-coloured belly, sooty webbed hindfeet, and a fine filament protruding from the tip of its tail. Like the great crested newt, it produces an aphrodisiac scent which it wafts towards the female by a frenzied fanning of the tail. The female can produce up to 350 eggs, which she fastens individually to the leaves of waterweeds.

Sometimes frogs also spawn in moorland quarry ponds, but usually they prefer small slow-running streams and seasonal puddles to permanent pools. Perhaps the risk of a drought is outweighed by fear of the aquatic predators which are likely to lurk in deeper water.

Huge mounds of spoil (*below*) add another dimension to the wildlife of an abandoned quarry. Orchids are often among the first plants to colonise such places. The type of the rock, in this case a lowland limestone quarry, is reflected in the vigorous plant growth.

Since most quarries are isolated from other wetlands by surrounding walls, the easiest access is by air. Dragonflies often venture far afield and in this way discover and colonise new ponds. During warm dry days in midsummer, adult dragonflies emerge, find a mate and breed before the weather breaks. The common hawker and the darter both have regular beats, skirting the ponds and hovering before returning to a favourite perch. In contrast the black darter is a restless creature flying a few metres, briefly settling, and then taking off again. Dragonflies seldom survive as winged adults for more than a few weeks. They may be beaten to the ground by heavy rain or taken by birds, the largest and most spectacular being the occasional visiting hobby. The nymphs live much longer, taking two years or more to reach full size.

Dragonfly nymphs hunt by either actively stalking their prey or relying on camouflage to keep them hidden as they lie in wait in the peaty silt which overlies the granite bottom. Many young newts fall victim to the sudden grasp of a nymph, and the young dragonflies themselves are not immune from attack. Cannibalism is common, both within and between different species. Many other animals also prey on nymphs, including herons and full-grown frogs. While the movement of a large hawker dragonfly nymph is usually slow and painstakingly deliberate, it can flee a predator with remarkable speed. Nymphs survive underwater by alternately contracting and expanding the abdomen to push a constant current of water through a rear vent into a gill chamber. To escape from predators, they reverse this system and expel water suddenly through the rear vent so that they shoot forward under aquatic jet propulsion.

As I climbed up a series of old well-worn steps on a clear day, the view from Haytor was stunning with a rich green rolling landscape stretching far below. This surface veneer of plant growth veils the underlying structure that gives shape to the ground. Scattered across the countryside I could see the man-made scars that reveal those rocks. Not all the quarries in the area yield solid stone. Vast quarries have been excavated deep into the lowlands to obtain huge quantities of the materials that help to hold together and support the structure of modern society – sand and gravel. These quarries have exposed the bed of an ancient river which flowed in Eocene times, some 70 million years ago in the aftermath of the dinosaurs. On a hot summer's day, the dry sandy surfaces bake in the sun and shimmer with heat. Few plants can survive in such arid conditions and even fewer animals. Yet in the topmost tier of one pit's massive steps, a soft sandy layer was being dug, not by hand but by foot.

The sand martin is the smallest of our three swallows, and generally the earliest to arrive. Chattering, interweaving flocks appear by the end of March in most years. Flying low over the water they hunt for aerial insects, such as mosquitoes and small flies. Although they are often seen over ponds and rivers, their nests are not necessarily located near water. They are colonial birds, which nest in burrows excavated in vertical banks. The colonies are usually small with 10 to 50 pairs nesting close together, but the numbers can grow to several hundred when populations are high. Their need for a suitable sandy face for burrowing seems to restrict their breeding range, and they are absent from large areas of chalk and limestone country in south and east England.

The birds sometimes nest in sandy sea-cliffs and river banks but by far the largest numbers breed in man-made sites. Sand martins do not select abandoned quarries left for nature to return. Instead, it is working quarries that attract the birds back year after year, as fresh excavations expose new vertical faces for the birds to exploit. Even the close proximity of people and noisy machines does not seem to deter them. Some colonies have been established in piles of quarry dust close to the grinding roar of a stone-crushing plant. Any loss of nest sites is rarely due to quarrying for the workers usually become interested in the welfare of 'their' birds.

Activity at the colony is sporadic. One minute the birds are clinging to the cliff and filling the air with a continual excited chatter, and the next, they have gone. Breeding begins with the excavation of new holes or the repair of the previous year's work. A tunnel up to a metre in length is driven into the cliff by both males and females using their tiny feet to scratch away the sand. Sometimes more than one tunnel is dug from a single entrance, and so a count of holes may not reveal an accurate number of nests.

A pair excavate a chamber at the end of the tunnel, and here the female lays four or five white eggs in a nest lined with grass and feathers. These are gathered in flight, as martins seldom if ever settle on the ground. Successful pairs may rear up to three broods each season, before leaving at the end of summer for their long flight south.

The sand martin population in Britain was thriving until the end of 1968, but when they returned the following spring their numbers were found to have crashed to around one quarter. Ringing studies of birds have revealed that they spend the winter months in Africa, south of the Sahara, and it is thought that drought in the Sahel region of Africa was responsible for their decline. With fewer insects to feed on, far less martins survive their trans-Saharan flight. The large chattering colonies that once flocked around quarry faces have now been reduced to only a few birds. If in the future climatic conditions once more favour the birds, there will be sandy horizons here waiting to be colonised.

Below The uncommon pyramidal orchid (*top*) grows typically on chalky soils, and thrives on a rocky ledge high in a limestone quarry. Herb robert (*bottom*) is an abundant flower found on walls and banks – often growing from just a small gap in the stone. *Opposite* Red valerian, originally a garden plant, now grows wild on walls and rocks.

The gravels mined in these south Devon quarries were laid down as freshwater river deposits. Nearby there are far more ancient beds, which owe their origin to the sea. The marine deposits did not form in cool temperate waters such as those that surround present-day Britain, but in the clear, shallow, tropical seas that covered the area about 400 million years ago.

This period of the Earth's history is called the Devonian after the county in which sediments of that age were first found. During the Devonian period the first forests of giant tree ferns grew, and primitive amphibians emerged on to a land largely devoid of animals. The seas, however, were teeming with life. A shower of shells and skeletons of marine organisms constantly drifted down to form a layer of sediment on the sea bed. Coral reefs grew and added their carcasses to the sediment. Over millions of years the countless remains accumulated, creating vast deposits. These compacted and hardened into a sedimentary rock known as limestone, which is composed chiefly of calcium carbonate.

Forces within the Earth caused movement of the Earth's crust, as they still do today, and the sea bed rose up into vast mountains. The sedimentary limestones were folded and tilted, even thrust on end and laid upside down. The tremendous pressures also created cracks and deep fissures within the rock. Limestone is a relatively soft rock and can be dissolved by the action of acids. Falling rain combines with carbon dioxide in the atmosphere to form a weak solution of carbonic acid. Over millions of years this gradually dissolved the rock, enlarging cracks and exploiting weaknesses. The water carried with it grit and soil debris, which further eroded the limestone, carving out passageways and galleries through it. Where these met and crossed each other, large chambers formed. As more rocks were dissolved and carried away by the water, some tunnels were undermined and collapsed causing further enlargement of the caves.

In limestone areas of the country streams can suddenly disappear into the ground. Some emerge at a lower level while others seem to have been swallowed up. Down through the millennia, such streams have literally eaten their way underground, creating entire systems of caves. From the slopes of Yorkshire to the Mendip hills there are spectacular series of caverns and passageways, extending for many kilometres underground. As the climate, land and river levels changed, the caves flooded or dried out. Periods of prolonged droughts and years of torrents are indelibly etched in the rock, and in the river-washed muds that eventually fill many systems.

The soft fine structure of limestone makes it easy to work, and so it has been much sought after. Blocks of rock are used in building, while the crushed rock provides support for many structures. Limestone is also heated in kilns to extract lime, which is used in building construction, glass manufacture and agriculture. Long before quarrying began, limestone provided the earliest known dwellings in Britain. Neanderthal people began occupying caves just before the last ice age, around 130 000 years ago, and people continued to use them as a refuge until 2000 years ago. Caves certainly have some advantages over simple man-made shelters. They are easily defended and provide a relatively constant temperature that fluctuates little throughout the year, remaining comparatively warm in a freezing winter and cool during the summer.

Little evidence remains today of the cave dwellers' way of life, and it is only through quarrying that many other cave systems have been opened up to us. Quarrying had already destroyed many sites before their importance was realised, and even when evidence was found it was initially ignored. The first recorded excavation of a British cave was conducted in 1816 by a contractor quarrying stone to build the nearby Plymouth breakwater. Numerous animal bones were carefully recovered along with several human remains. In those days it was thought that ancient animals and modern people had never lived together in the same area, let alone at the same time. So the human remains were considered irrelevant and were tipped over a cliff.

Stone implements have been found in caves that were spared from quarrying. Dating has shown that one of these, Kent's Cavern in Torquay, is the oldest inhabited British cave. In some caverns, the only evidence of past occupation is the charred remains of a few stone-age fires. In others, relics, including animal and plant fossils, have provided a tantalising glimpse of past life.

Long before Higher Kiln quarry at Buckfastleigh in Devon was abandoned nearly a century ago, it was known that there were caves in the area. However, it was not until 1939 that these were first explored by some enthusiastic young cavers. The tiny air movements from caverns can be sufficient to bend a flame in the confines of a tunnel, and the cavers found their way by following the flickering light of candles. Wriggling, crawling and digging through narrow passages they came across huge caves with bizarrely shaped deposits covering the roofs and walls. Spectacular though these were, their most remarkable find lay in a cave called Joint Mitnor. This was filled to the roof by a mound, or talus cone, of earth and rock rubble. Over the following two years, excavations unearthed some 4000 bones and teeth, the richest assemblage of mammal remains yet found in a British cave. It included the remains of exotic species, such as hippopotamus, narrow-nosed rhinoceros, straight-tusked elephant, bison, cave lion, hyena, bear and giant deer, along with pig, badger, fallow and red deer, wolf, fox, wild cat and hare.

The variety of wildlife in an old quarry depends as much on its age and the type of rock as on the nature of the surrounding country. Moorland pools in flooded granite quarries contain relatively little life – the keeled skimmer dragonfly (*below*) and the palmate newt (*bottom*) both breed in quarry ponds such as this one at Haytor.

Early investigations suggested that the roof of Joint Mitnor had collapsed leaving a hole into which the occasional animal fell, but more recent research has revealed a different explanation. Some remains still lie in one corner of the cave. For me the most poignant is the first tooth and scattered bones of a baby prehistoric elephant. Looking closely at some of the bones it is possible to see the teeth marks of a cave hyena. It now appears that a long narrow rift extended up to the surface, providing access to the cave. While some animals may have just fallen in, others were probably dragged or carried there after being scavenged by hyenas. Even the pathways that they followed along the cave floor have been found.

The finds at Joint Mitnor and other caves give a vivid picture of the wildlife that roamed this country between 120 000 and 18 000 years ago. Before this period, Britain was in the grip of an ice age, and arctic conditions prevailed. Gradually the ice age receded and the climate became much warmer than it is today. This allowed animals from the south to migrate north and colonise new ground. Some 20 000 years ago, the warm temperate climate began to end and the country was on the long slide back into another ice age. This continued for about 10 000 years, with a series of brief climatic reprieves. During this time, successive falls of rock and rubble in Joint Mitnor brought down and buried more bones, until eventually the cave was sealed by the rising mound. Over the past 10 000 years, a hard stalagmite layer has slowly formed across its surface, deposited by lime-laden water dripping from the roof.

Today the Dart meanders where once a wide hippo-inhabited river flowed. Its surface level has dropped slowly over the years, leaving the caves high, if not entirely dry. During the heavy winter rains water seeps in through the multitude of cracks and crevices permeating the rocks above. It flows down the walls and even sprays under pressure from hairline fractures. The trickling streams eventually merge to form raging torrents tumbling through the darkness. Such periodic flooding maintains deep lakes within some caves. Across the valley from Joint Mitnor lie two of the deepest underground lakes so far found in this country. In one of them, Pridhamsleigh, people have dived down to 36 metres, close to the limits of their equipment. At this depth the dark water disappears into a dense impenetrable mud, and the actual lake bottom may be far below.

Water, the original architectural agent of the caves, continues to furnish their interiors. As it passes through the rock, the water becomes heavily laden with lime. Some of this is deposited as calcite, covering the ceiling, walls and floor in extraordinary shapes and colours. In upper-level caves, long since deserted by streams, dripping water leaves a series of calcite rings on the ceilings. Over thousands of years, the rings develop into tubular stalactites which slowly fill to become solid. Any excess solution of calcite drips through the interminable darkness to leave a deposit on the floor. Because the solution splashes on the ground, the stalagmite that forms is thicker and grows more slowly than its twin structure above. In some caves, the stalactites from the ceiling have reached the stalagmites growing from the floor, creating pillars. The speed of growth of calcite structures varies. Some cave stalactites have been estimated to grow little more than 25 millimetres in a thousand years. In contrast, one hanging in an abandoned mine elsewhere is already the length of a man in less than a century.

I negotiated with difficulty a long, winding passage in the upper levels of a cave system, which eventually widened into a small grotto. There in the light of my headlamp stood the shape of a figure, arms stretched, and apparently wearing a top hat. It is thought that such strange shapes may have been produced by periodic flooding causing fluctuating water levels. Air moving through the caves can also distort the growing calcite, producing structures with bends and hooks called helic-tites or helic-mites.

Some galleries are adorned with hanging limestone curtains formed by water trickling from small fissures in the roof. Where water flows across wide areas of rock it deposits flowstone. Crystal pools grow where lime-saturated water is trapped in small basins, before seasonally drying out. Around other pools, a growing edge of rimstone may form. Even grit or small grains of material can become coated, and these are known as cave pearls. In caves containing air saturated with moisture, the walls become covered with a soft calcium crystal called moonmilk. Calcite structures are often white or pearly but may take on different hues in areas where the water passes through other materials besides limestone. Iron colours calcite red, copper turns it a shade of green, while manganese gives it a black tinge.

Walking into a cave on a warm summer's day, the temperature and light level drops abruptly. Beyond the threshold of the bright world outside, sun-loving plants can no longer survive, and even the shade-tolerant ferns and mosses gradually give way to bare rock. However, even the darkest of caves can support a variety of life. In such conditions only a limited ability to detect light from dark is necessary to survive, and skin colour serves no useful purpose. As a result, cave-dwelling species often lack any pigment and are virtually blind. Some cave pools support a tiny community of freshwater gammarid shrimps and a lively little copepod relation, living in total blackness. Most other cave dwellers are found closer to the entrance. In the dim light, attractive pink or pure white woodlice forage on the floor, along with small beetles and tiny springtails, which pass unnoticed by all but a few.

On a hot summer's day, the temperature in a sand and gravel quarry can soar. Such desert-like conditions are attractive to very few creatures, but in the steep upper faces a colony of sand martins have excavated their nests. The majority of these birds in Britain now breed in man-made cliffs.

The cave spider is the only British species found exclusively in such cool dark surroundings. In one small but aptly named cave, Spider's Hole, they hang motionless on a few strands of web waiting for a passing meal. The female spins a large silken sac containing eggs, which is suspended from the ceiling by a short stalk. Protected from cold dripping water and other spiders, the young hatchlings eventually eat their way out. Although not common, cave spiders are widespread. Since adults are seldom, if ever, found outside the entrance of caves, it is thought that it must be the young spiderlings which colonise new caves.

Autumn and winter brings new life to the caves, as creatures seek a refuge in which to pass the coldest months literally in suspended animation – hanging from the walls. The most colourful is the herald moth, which seeks out a dry recess before settling down. Here it remains hibernating until the following spring. Gnats, craneflies and some mosquitoes spend the winter in caves, protected from bitter winds, rain and snow. The shelter and constant temperature of caves also attract another much larger creature, sometimes in considerable numbers.

Few insects can be found during the winter, and so in early autumn the bats increase their weight and draw on these food reserves while hibernating from October until April. Of the eight species of bat that inhabit caves, only the greater and lesser horseshoe can be found in large numbers. Today up to 500 may share a single roost, but in the past, when bats were far more common, the colonies may have been much bigger.

Bats are the only mammals capable of sustained flight, moving so fast and agilely through the air that it can be difficult for the human eye to follow them. The wings of a bat are tough, despite their fragile appearance. The thin membranous skin is supported by arms with elongated digits. In British bats, the thumb is armed with a needle-sharp claw, as is each of the toes. Another feature distinguishing bats from the rest of the mammals is a backward-bending knee. Their bodies are covered and kept warm by a soft dense fur, which they spend hours grooming each day.

All British bats feed on insects which they catch in flight, over water or land. During the summer they consume vast numbers, including many crop pests, on their nightly foraging flights. One of the smallest of the 15 species of bat found in this country, the pipistrelle, is estimated to eat over 3500 insects each night. The much larger greater horseshoe bat is named after a complex series of skin folds which form a U-shape around its nostrils. The folds concentrate the high-pitched sound produced by the bat into a narrow beam, with which the bat scans the area around it. By listening to the echoes of the sound reflected from the surroundings, the bat can build up a sound picture of the area. Using this echo-location system, it can detect a moth flying through the air or a beetle scuttling along the ground. Some insects are caught in the jaws, while others are scooped out of the air by a wing or tail membrane, before being transferred to the mouth. Cockchafers and maybugs are eagerly sought, as are craneflies and larger moths, but most prey is probably far smaller.

Bats are intelligent sociable creatures with a relatively long life, up to 30 years, and this is reflected in the time it takes them to mature. They do not breed until their second to fourth year. Although mating occurs during the autumn, fertilisation is delayed until spring and the young bats are born in midsummer. The greater horseshoe bat establishes its nursery roost in a warmer location than the hibernation cave, often using an old building. The females are usually four or sometimes even five years old before they give birth to a single, rarely twin, young. The mother tends her baby closely, suckling frequently both day and night. At three weeks, the young bats make their first flights and two weeks later they are weaned.

At the end of summer the horseshoe bats return to their chosen cave. It may have been selected for a variety of reasons including high humidity, but temperature and lack of disturbance are probably the most important. Many negotiate narrow twisting tunnels to winter roosts a long way inside. Some colonies roost in large easily accessible caves, and in the past these have suffered from both intentional and accidental disturbance. Awakening during hibernation burns vital energy supplies and several disturbances may cause death. Bats have also been killed by fire or suffocated by smoke. Others have fallen to sticks and stones, or been shot at in the air by rifles, forming easy targets as they hang in a deep winter sleep. Several well-known bat caves have therefore been fitted with metal grilles, which have sufficient space between the bars to allow the bats to enter in flight.

In October, deciduous trees respond to the shortening, colder days by shedding their leaves. Some bats are still making short forays in the chill night air, in a last attempt to catch a few flying insects before they too succumb to the cold. Deep inside the cave the activity of early autumn has become quieter as the bats prepare for winter. All true hibernating mammals must undergo a period of preparation for their deep sleep. The first stage is a marked increase in body weight as they build up reserves of fat. Unlike migratory birds which overeat and store the excess, bats do not appear to increase the frequency of their catches. Instead, they spend an increasing part of the day in torpor and so convert less of the food they eat into energy, storing the tiny surplus as a layer of fat. In this way,

Carved by water over thousands of years, a limestone cave provides a home for some special creatures. *Below* A cave spider protects its young in a silken cocoon. The greater horseshoe bat (*bottom*) hibernates through winter and the herald moth (*opposite bottom*) also passes the coldest months inside. Stalactites hang from the roof and other formations line the walls and form crystal pools.

they slowly accumulate over a quarter of their body weight as a reserve to see them through the winter.

The triggers for the onset of hibernation are not well understood, but shortage of food, reduced day length, and dropping temperatures probably all play a part. Once a bat has found a secure foothold its body processes begin to decline. With its wings wrapped around its body the vital functions slow down. Unlike other mammals, the bat's body temperature fluctuates widely, reaching up to 42 degrees Centigrade in flight and falling to 10 degrees Centigrade while digesting a meal. At rest the body temperature may become the same as that of the surroundings, and while in winter sleep it approaches close to freezing. Some species of bat, when active, have a heart rate approaching 1000 beats a minute. In hibernation that can fall to a mere 20. The blood flow to the skin is closed in a bid to conserve what little heat remains, and even the composition of the blood changes as the red cells reduce in number. When in deep sleep, the bat's breathing is barely discernible and it hangs close to death.

Although hibernation is a survival strategy, allowing the bats to escape the rigours of winter, it is not without its risks and some individuals will perish. The young of the year are particularly vulnerable because they commit a large proportion of their first summer's food to simply growing. They are often the last to enter hibernation as they make a final bid to build up their reserves and, even so, may lay down insufficient fat to last them through the coldest months. In late winter some bats will take advantage of any warm spell to hunt insects which will sustain them for a few more vital weeks. However, the food reserves of most hibernating bats are just enough to see them through to the spring, without much margin for error.

With the arrival of warm weather, a bat can awake from months of sleep and warm to an active temperature in less than 20 minutes. It is usually dusk when the first bats venture from the cave to begin their night-time hunt. During their active summer, they are still far from safe. In the early hours of one summer's morning, I was watching a brood of tawny owl chicks, when the parent bird entered the tree with a small bat hanging from its beak. From the eager way it was taken by an owlet, and from bones found in pellets, it was obvious that bats are a familiar catch for the tawny owl. The barn owl, too, will take the occasional bat. This is hardly surprising as old buildings, such as those found in quarries, are frequented as much by barn owls as by bats. Even before there were barns, these white owls probably sought the shelter of caves along with the bats.

Birds which hunt during the day, such as the kestrel, can also pose a threat. As darkness falls, the familiar outline of this common falcon may be seen hovering in the fading light, especially if food is scarce and it still has young to feed. Although not a regular kill, kestrels will catch the occasional bat that emerges early. Kestrels nest in a hole or on a ledge high on a rock face, and have taken to the man-made cliff faces of quarries. On a late summer afternoon, the quarry walls can ring to the sound of their chanting calls as they fly and follow each other. With grass-covered land above them and scree slopes at their feet, they do not have to travel far for a hunting ground. From the vantage point of a tree or a prominent ledge, they peer intently before pouncing on a grasshopper or cricket. Insects make up a large proportion of the diet of some birds of prey. However, the kestrel is more often seen with its tail fanned out and wings beating vigorously as it hovers in wait for voles and mice. Dropping in steps closer to the ground, it takes its victim by surprise rather than by speed.

Though capable of fast flight, the kestrel is out-classed in the chase by a spectacular killer, the peregrine falcon. The peregrine soars in the sky above its hunting territory at a distance far too remote to seem menacing. On sighting prey, such as a passing pigeon, it swoops with partly closed wings reaching a speed estimated at 290 kilometres an hour. At such a velocity, it closes on its victim in seconds, striking with such devastating force that the prey's neck is often broken by the blow.

Recent years have witnessed a remarkable come back of this bird. From the turn of the century until 1939, some 700 peregrines bred in Britain and Ireland, nesting on inland crags and sea cliffs. The nest sites or eyries are traditional and, in some cases, their occupation can be traced back to the Middle Ages. For centuries, peregrines were highly prized by falconers. Then, with the introduction of the sporting gun, the persecution of this falcon began.

It officially reached a peak during the Second World War, when some 600 peregrines were killed to protect carrier pigeons delivering vital messages. After the war their numbers slowly revived, only to fall again from 1956. This decline in population was the first sign that the birds were being killed insidiously by agricultural pesticides. Increasing numbers of broken eggs were found, including many that were infertile, and the numbers of peregrines crashed. In the last decade, a partial ban on the use of some persistent pesticides has led to a recovery. The peregrine is once again returning to traditional eyries and even seeking out more recently created sites in old and abandoned quarries – perhaps the first step in nature's slow recolonisation of these bare grounds.

CHAPTER 5

BEYOND THE BARBED WIRE

As dawn broke over Dartmoor, a heavy drizzle shielded the distant hills from view and soaked the heather-clad slopes. This wild windswept scene seemed as untouched by people as any place in Britain. Then from the valley floor a flare rose in an arc, and the distant rumbles of rotor blades announced the arrival of two helicopters. They thundered past, hugging the hillside low in the valley before rising and settling to disgorge their troops. The military exercise unfolding before my eyes was momentarily lost in the smoke of gunfire and exploding shells. Yet amongst all the commotion of noise and fighting men, a skylark sang from the sky.

Strange as it may seem, some of the finest and rarest species in the country inhabit areas which are used as battlegrounds. The Ministry of Defence is one of Britain's largest landowners, having currently about 240 000 hectares directly under its control. This land is held in trust for the nation, and in 1973 the Ministry appointed an officer to administer and encourage its conservation. The first task was to survey the land and examine and catalogue its wildlife. As a result, around 200 sites of special scientific interest have been identified within Ministry of Defence boundaries, and today some 5000 dedicated service and civilian volunteers have 182 000 hectares under their care. The sites include grasslands which have remained untouched for more than 200 years, about 340 kilometres of spectacular coastline, and some of the finest regions of national parks.

The survey revealed that nearly all Britain's rare and uncommon wild animals and plants are at home on the ranges. The flora was found to be especially rich, and includes such notable species as the coralroot orchid and tree mallow which has rarely been recorded anywhere else in the country, and the grape hyacinth and maiden pink, which had not been seen in Britain since 1887. Stretches of snowdrops, fields of cowslips and woodlands carpeted with bluebells produce spectacular seasonal displays. Yet for sheer beauty few flowers can compare with the weird and wonderful blooms produced by the bee and fen orchids, all of which are found within MoD boundary fences.

Almost as impressive are the quantity and variety of birds. All three services have active bird-watching societies, and civilians have added numerous sightings to the steadily growing lists. Rarities, such as the stone curlew, hobby and Dartford warbler, are well represented, as are redstart, nightjar, nightingale and woodlark. Ministry of Defence lands also contain one of the largest little tern colonies in Europe. Many of these species leave at the end of summer, but others arrive to take their place. In winter, birds settle on the coastal ranges and mud flats at Foulness, including brent geese, common scoters and hen harriers.

The smooth snake and the sand lizard are the rarest reptiles in the country and are protected by law. In addition, several of their sites are under the guard of the military. The equally uncommon natterjack toad has been found on four ranges, one of which is its only outpost in the south of Britain. Bats, too, need all the protection that can be afforded them. The Royal Air Force depot at Chilmark is well known for its caves and quarries, which were the source of stone for the building of Salisbury cathedral, but perhaps less appreciated is the area's importance for bats. Of the 15 species native to the British Isles, 10 are found here, including large colonies of greater and lesser horseshoe bats.

The ranges are home to all six types of deer found in Britain and contain perhaps the largest single populations of the now naturalised sika and muntjac in the entire country. However, it is probably the smallest animals which benefit most from the protection of the armed services. Away from the widespread use of chemical pest and weed control, the insects thrive. In a survey of 11 sites, over 30 species of butterflies were recorded, including the rare black hairstreak, marsh fritillary and Essex skipper, along with the attractive Duke of Burgundy butterfly and the Glanville fritillary. So far little work has been done on moths, but 437 different species have already been listed on one site alone.

Because of the danger from bullets and exploding shells, the public obviously has to be kept clear of the surrounding areas while military operations are in progress. Even when the training is over, access must still remain limited because of the presence of unexploded rounds. The exclusion of people from these areas of countryside is of huge benefit to the wildlife. Cattle and sheep are allowed to graze on some ranges, which does little to disturb the land and, indeed, maintains the floral richness of ancient pasture. In other more sensitive sites, such as those of particular natural or archaeological interest, even troops and farming are restricted and the wildlife is left largely in peace and seclusion.

At the end of the Second World War, nearly 5 million hectares were under Ministry of Defence control. Today, a large proportion of that has been handed back to the nation, but the armed forces' need for land is greater than ever before. Over the last 20 years more and more troops have been stationed at home rather than overseas, and handling sophisticated weapons requires extensive training.

The resultant pressure on the 240 000 hectares of land remaining has not, however, been as bad for the environment as might be supposed. The armed forces have powerful reasons to conserve the natural and agricultural character of the ranges. Infantry cannot train realistically on barren, bomb-scarred and shell-cratered land and the progress of tanks would be impeded, while artillery practice would be too easy without tree cover.

Careful management keeps the ranges looking like other comparable areas outside, which benefits both the armed services and the wildlife. The natural value of the ranges can also be enhanced in unexpected ways. For example, if some of the craters excavated during artillery practice are not filled in, they will become flooded and provide a new freshwater habitat. Some pools have been created deliberately by directing the sappers' explosive skills towards a planned location. Within a few years, freshwater ponds in otherwise dry areas teem with life. Of the 37 species of dragonfly which currently breed on a regular basis in Britain, 27 have been identified on Ministry of Defence lands.

Some ranges see only occasional large-scale movements of troops and machines. In others, there are regular training exercises and firing occurs week after week. Wild animals cope remarkably well with such bombardments. Creatures can adapt to disturbances if they happen in the same places at the same times each day, and the armed services are renowned for their strict routines. The degree of military control exercised over an area varies according to its use. Some ranges are completely closed and protected by kilometres of barbed wire, while in most access is limited to obvious and often fenced paths.

In contrast, Dartmoor is a national park where people can walk virtually

Dartmoor is the largest area of true wilderness left in England and has been a national park since 1951. But for nearly 200 years it has also been used by the military. Ponies (*opposite*) are a familiar feature, while cotton grass (*inset*) grows in the wettest parts.

anywhere they like, except on firing days. Dartmoor is the largest true wilderness left in England, covering over 1000 square kilometres, and is of national importance for wildlife. This wild rugged land contains heathlands with rough grazing, valley mires and vast blanket bog. The highest ground is covered with cotton grass moor or bog. The rainfall of 2 metres or more each year makes these uplands among the wettest in the country. Yet there are only a few areas of open water, such as Cranmere pool, which usually dries up in the summer. The sponge-like nature of the moors is due to its thick blanket of sphagnum moss and the rotten granite below which soak up much of the rainfall. From around the central plateau, trickles of water are slowly released and form small young streams. Tumbling down over granite boulders, the bubbling waters merge into miniature torrents, swirling around rock-lined pools before continuing their descent. In the valleys the streams join to form rivers, which spread and slow in middle age until they eventually meander into the sea. Five of the largest rivers in Devon begin from the blanket bog on the high moor.

The first recorded use of Dartmoor by the military was during the Napoleonic wars in 1805, but it was not until 1896 that regular troop training began there. In those days a manoeuvre could involve 12 000 men and 2000 horses. The exercises today are small in comparison, with movements of an entire battalion of about 600 men being few and far between. However, there is regular firing of small arms and light artillery on the ranges. Over 100 square kilometres of the moors are licensed for military use, covering Okehampton, Willsworthy and Merrivale ranges. These areas are mainly on the north and west moor straddling High Willhays tor which, at 621 metres, is the highest point on the moors. The borders of the ranges are well marked in many places by the traditional granite walls that criss-cross the lower slopes. Up on the high, open moor, red flags serve as a long distance warning, with chequered marker posts set in between.

Dartmoor supports many fascinating mountain and moorland species, although in winter the dead, bleached grass can give an impression of barrenness. During this season the moor presents a dramatic windswept landscape, especially when lit by a low sun against dark grey clouds. The view can disappear with frightening speed as the mists for which the moors are famous descend. Then only the occasional call of a raven or crow breaks the sound of the wind.

Spring comes late to the moor and with the arrival of warm weather and longer days the scene changes. On the slopes above the valley bogs the haunting calls of curlew carry on the breeze and over the mire a drumming announces the return of the snipe. The curious noise of these summer visitors to the moors is not a vocal call but the sound produced as they dive through the air. Two outer tail feathers, one on each side, are stiffer than the rest. The bird dives at an angle of about 45 degrees and holds these feathers straight out from its body. The air rushing past makes the feathers vibrate, creating a resonant bleat. Although the drumming may be heard at any time of year, it is most frequently part of the bird's courtship display in spring and early summer, and seems to fulfil the same function as song, declaring territory and attracting a mate. Snipe are usually found in wetlands where they probe with their long bills for worms and other small creatures underground. The beak makes up a quarter of the bird's body length and its flexible, sensitive tip enables the snipe to feel for its wriggling prey.

A more familiar sound from the edge of the mire is that of the peewit calling its name. This handsome dark green, chestnut and white bird with a distinctive feather crest is better known as the lapwing. Like those of the snipe, its young are well developed on hatching and leave the nest within a few hours. In the breeding season, the lapwing becomes bold and will mob passing crows and buzzards while continually uttering its plaintive cry. This distracts predators from the nest and may also teach the young to recognise their natural enemies.

On the highest plateau, a few golden plover and dunlin may nest each year, and where heather still grows a small number of red grouse may survive. By far the most vocal birds of these uplands are the skylarks. The males hover in the breeze above their nesting territory while pouring out their song. Like the meadow pipit, skylarks build nests close to the ground, hidden in a tussock of grass. However most birds avoid the exposed high ground and seek the lee of rocks and valleys.

In some parts of the moor, old tin mines have left a maze of channels and spoil heaps now covered by turf which give shelter to breeding birds. The wheatear winters in Africa and returns in the summer to nest on high ground, often in a rock cleft or hole in a wall. The much rarer ring ousel is another migrant, arriving from Africa in late spring to breed on Britain's mountains and moors. It looks just like a garden blackbird but has paler wings and a striking white crescent on its breast. Its character is also quite distinct, for it is shy and difficult to approach.

The variety of bird life on the moors is limited by the fact that food is scarce for much of the year. The insect life is similarly restricted and consists mainly of strong flying species, such as bumble bees and butterflies, visiting from lower ground or passing through on migration. The heather and ling that are so characteristic of the upland heath are among the few species to thrive in such dry, peaty soil.

Where the drainage of rainwater is in some way impeded, the vegetation becomes far richer. Cross-leaved heath grows in place of the more familiar

Bogs are treacherous places but full of fascinating plants. Sphagnum moss (*below left*) plays a key role in the creation of the bog. Bogbean (*below, main picture and inset*) and bog myrtle (*opposite, inset top*) are common flowers. Others, such as the butterwort (*opposite, main picture*) and sundew (*opposite, inset bottom*), are carnivorous.

heather, along with rushes, cotton grass and purple moor-grass. Lower down in the valleys, damp areas may be carpeted with the rich green growth of sphagnum and other plants. Adult dragonflies are seen around the bogs and along streams during summer. The valley mires especially support a more varied flora and with it a greater variety of insect larvae consuming the leaves of plants.

One of the most curious features of a mire is that its centre may stand 6 or 7 metres higher than its edges. Known as a raised bog, such a mound is formed when successive layers of peat build up over the years, lifting the surface of the bog above the surrounding water level. This transforms an acid bog, in which only heathers and mosses tolerant of such impoverished conditions can survive, into a rich and fragile island. Stepping carefully out into this soggy realm, the ground quaked beneath my feet. I moved slowly from one dry tussock to another, until I surmounted the dome of a raised bog. Its remarkable plant community, surviving for thousands of years untrampled by moorland livestock, included bog bean, bog myrtle and the spectacular little sundew. This carnivorous plant can grow in nutrient-deficient ground by extracting the substances it needs from insect life. Its rosette of red-tinged leaves carries glistening rings of tentacles which cause any small insect alighting to come literally to a sticky end. The tentacles respond to the movements of struggling prey by slowly curling inwards and the plant gradually absorbs the insect's vital elements. The less common butterwort is another insectivorous plant. Its fleshy leaves curl inwards along their length to absorb tiny creatures trapped on their sticky surfaces.

The raised bogs which harbour such extraordinary life forms are not without their dangers, and Dartmoor is reputed to contain bogs several metres deep. Most are quite shallow, but it is still possible to break through the sodden layer of moss into water below, and even the dry tussocks may contain a venomous adder basking in the sun. In such ground, the bog asphodel, also known as the 'bone breaker', raises its yellow flowering spike. Contrary to popular belief, this plant does not harm grazing cattle and sheep. Its presence is merely an indicator of lime-poor boglands where livestock should not be grazed.

Dartmoor's upland soil, often waterlogged and acidic, excludes the earthworm and one of its principal predators, the mole. The only common mollusc of these calcium-deficient soils is the large and ponderous great black slug. Where the undergrowth is dense, however, a good beetle population can survive. These insects are an important source of food for many animals including the badger, which consumes hundreds of beetles in a night. Insects are also the main prey of the common and pygmy shrews, both of which hunt in the area. We can hear only the lowest notes of these small mammals' calls because their vocal range extends into the ultrasonic. In late summer, the sound of their high-pitched shrieks combines with the incessant strident tones of grasshoppers and crickets flanking the moorland path.

Although butterflies and moths are not always obvious on the moor, several species can be seen in August. The fox, emperor and oak eggar moths, and the meadow brown and gatekeeper butterflies, are not uncommon, while the grayling occurs in some areas. The caterpillars of these insects provide food for many birds. Apart from insects there is very little prey for larger animals. Kestrels and even foxes and badgers are known to take voles, but the moorland life provides a rather meagre diet for these larger predators, so most also rely on scavenging. The richest pickings are found among the still-born lambs and sheep which finally succumb to the harsh regime of the high moors.

Foxes often rear their young on the clitter slopes where a scattering of massive rocks prevents easy access. They appear undisturbed by the background clatter of automatic gunfire or the distant thud of artillery, which occasionally continues both day and night. Holding training sessions involving live ammunition within a national park is a contentious issue. Many birds and mammals regularly breed on the Dartmoor ranges. The armed exercises are under strict controls and efforts are made to avoid sensitive areas, but some damage is unavoidable. However, according to the Nature Conservancy Council, the military causes little, if any, long-term harm to the wildlife. In contrast, the land management of the moors continues to pose a serious threat. For years, overgrazing and burning have been steadily destroying the nature of the land. Heather is becoming increasingly rare as it is replaced by rough grazing. In addition, there is growing pressure from people visiting Dartmoor for recreation. The number of walkers is increasing each year, including those people training for the annual long-distance ten-tors walk. While this event only lasts a few days and is carefully co-ordinated, the unsupervised training period spans the most critical time for many moorland nesting birds.

The incubation of eggs is an equally sensitive time for seabirds. Yet remarkably, birds thrive along the coastal firing range of HMS *Cambridge*. Situated south of the moors, off a beautiful stretch of the south Devon coast on the outer edge of Plymouth breakwater, HMS *Cambridge* is the only remaining naval gunnery school in Britain. It was commissioned in 1956, exactly 100 years after the wooden warship bearing the same name began its training work moored in the River Tamar. Now a shore-based station, HMS *Cambridge* occupies nearly a kilometre of coastline covering 60 hectares of land. Its firing range extends 21 kilometres out to sea and includes the Eddystone lighthouse. The rocky shore

Below Common moorland nesting birds include the lapwing (*top*) and the curlew (*bottom*). *Right* Young badger cubs spend hours play-fighting right next to the naval gunnery school of HMS *Cambridge*.

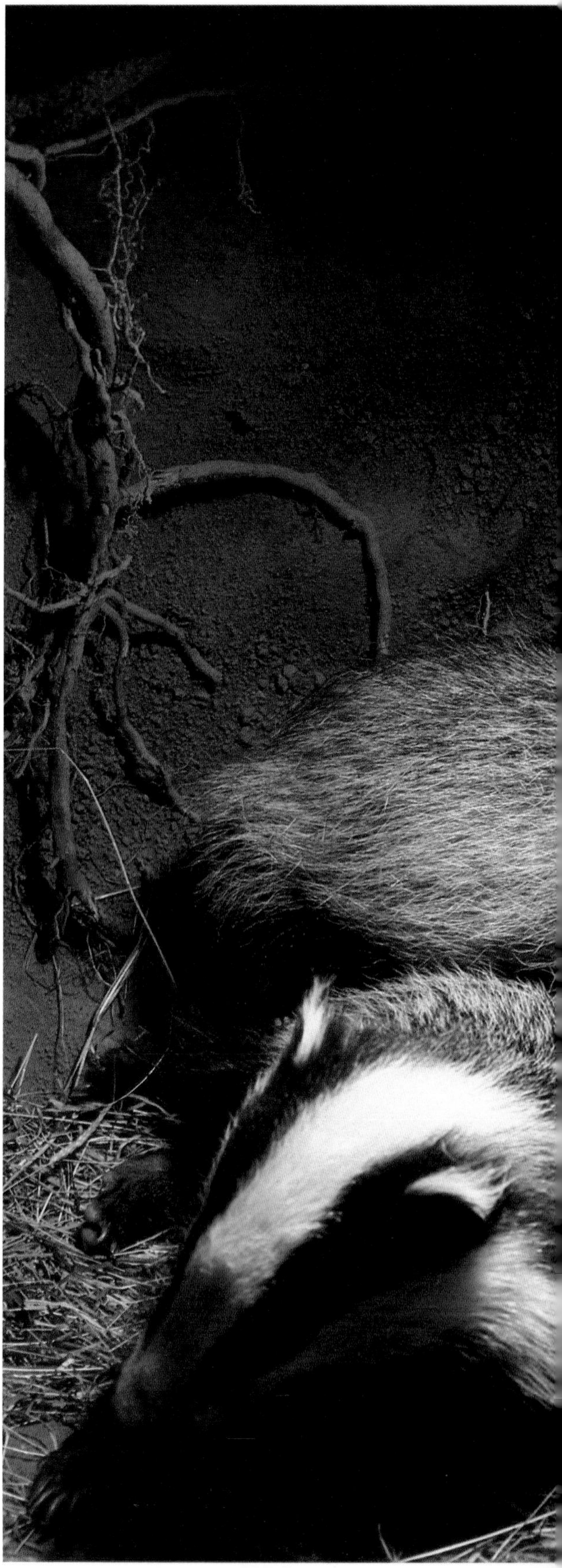

and low cliffs, draped with wild flowers in summer, are of stunning beauty, and the coastline is classified as a site of special scientific interest.

Low tide reveals a large foreshore with a series of raised rock ledges running out into the sea. In spring, when bird migration is at its height, this shore attracts a great number of turnstones. Though a few non-breeding birds may be present all year, most turnstones fly to the northernmost lands of the world to breed. In winter they migrate south to the Atlantic coasts of Britain and Europe or as far away as the southern tip of Africa, South America, Australia and New Zealand. They often appear as passage migrants in the company of other waders, such as dunlin, ringed plovers and purple sandpipers.

Turnstones gather in the largest concentrations where the good sustenance they need for their long flights is readily available. The richest pickings are to be found on rocky, stone-covered shores where seaweed hides an abundance of marine life. Their black, brown and white plumage looks striking against the blue sea, but renders them almost invisible on the rocky beach. Only their movements give them away as they sweep energetically over the shore, like an inquisitive mottled army, turning over small stones in search of small prey. Despite their name, they will move anything – shells, driftwood, dead fish or weed – which may conceal the sand hoppers, insects and small fish on which they feed.

Apart from the sound of gunfire echoing along the coast, to which the birds soon become accustomed, there is little to disturb their feeding. The area offshore is a voluntary marine reserve, the beach is little used and boats are not permitted to land. Although a coastal footpath winds its way over the cliffs, people are reminded by signs not to stray too far, especially on firing days.

The slope extending up behind the shore is covered in a dense impenetrable scrub consisting mainly of gorse. This area is of particular importance to thousands of migrating warblers which use it as a staging post to feed and shelter while on their spring and autumn passages. Many rarities have been spotted along this part of the coast, resting for a few days before continuing their wayward course. The elusive cirl bunting, a native of the Mediterranean, has even taken up residence. This bird is only found in the warmest parts of the country, in the south and west of England. More widespread and not nearly as shy, the closely related yellowhammer and the whitethroat also breed along this part of the coast.

As the sun sets over Plymouth Sound and seabirds fly past in line, the badgers set out along their trails which criss-cross the cliffs. Even the tall perimeter fences do not stop them for they tunnel underneath. They have dug deep into the slopes below the gunnery school, almost undermining the naval establishment. Incredible as it may seem for animals with such well-developed sense of smell and hearing, badgers appear to thrive within deafening range of the blast of the guns. By day they stay below ground, emerging under the cover of night to forage for beetles and grubs. However, badgers are omnivorous creatures and will seize any opportunity to exploit a new source of food. The naval night guard regularly encounters them raiding the bins from the mess.

HMS *Cambridge* is set in a sea of grass with waves of pink thrift, wild carrot and other summer flowers. It flies standard red flags to warn that live ammunition is being fired. A target is towed into the area, and operational procedures are followed to ensure a clear firing arc. Then the sound of loud guns echoes along the cliffs and out across the sea.

Small boats cruise and sail along the coast, despite the area being marked on navigation charts as a danger zone. If a boat sails into the area while firing is in progress, the gun crews must cease operations immediately. With live ammunition already loaded, the guns have to be pointed in a safe direction until the boat has crossed into safe waters. At such times, all guns are brought to bear on a large rock stack called the Mewstone, lying less than a kilometre off the mainland. Landing on the Mewstone is, therefore, restricted and it is uninhabited by people. But this has not always been the case. Historical records tell of an entire family that eked out a meagre living on this exposed rock for 100 years until 1840. The remains of their small stone house with its round window and steeply terraced grounds can still be seen. There is little evidence of any older occupation, but it is thought that the island may have been used in medieval times as a religious retreat or perhaps the site of a beacon.

Today the Mewstone is a sanctuary for seabirds protected by the Royal Navy and only rarely visited with special permission. The island is steep and even the previously inhabited south side proved a stiff climb. Tall stinging nettles thrived on the droppings of birds, and salt-tolerant plants gave a lush green covering to the slope. As I made my way up, the ground became carpeted by bluebells, looking strangely out of place in such bleak surroundings. Although they are normally considered to be plants of deciduous woods, bluebells thrive on many offshore islands and here their colours seemed to be particularly vivid. Clambering up through the tangle of plants, seagulls hung in the air, screaming if I passed too close to one of their nests. When I reached the top ridge, the landward side of the island fell steeply away in a series of cliffs with wide ledges. The sounds, smells and white excreta-splashed rocks are the mark of a large seabird colony. The Mewstone supports a great many nesting cormorants. It also has one of the largest populations of shag found around the southern coast, and is of national

Below The Mewstone just offshore is not only a safe bearing for the naval guns but also supports a large seabird colony, with cormorants breeding on a series of cliff ledges.
Opposite The Mewstone is also home to one of the largest colonies of nesting shags found along the south coast. Shag chicks remain in the nest for over seven weeks.

importance for these birds. Since the 1920s there has been a striking increase in the number of shag and they are one of Britain's fastest growing bird populations.

Both cormorants and shags occur all round the coast of Britain, apart from the south east. While shags remain at sea throughout the year, cormorants are commonly seen inland. Outside the breeding season, they make their way up estuaries and rivers to frequent lakes and reservoirs. The species are similar in appearance, but the cormorant's black plumage is relieved by a white chin. The adult shag is smaller with no white markings and bears a handsome crest when breeding.

These large birds can consume their own weight of fish in a day. They swim strongly underwater with their wings held tight to the body and their strong webbed feet driving them forward. The shag hunts in mid-water, catching free-swimming fish, mainly sand-eels. The cormorant tends to dive down in shallower water to feed on bottom-living flatfish. Once back on the surface, weighed down by a crop crammed full of fish, the birds need a long running take-off to become airborne. They then fly low over the waves back to the shore. After diving for fish and feeding, they can often be seen perched on rocks and buoys with wings outstretched. Unlike other web-footed birds, they do not produce a waterproofing oil for their plumage and must dry out their feathers between feeds.

The birds breed in a loose colony on ledges or in cavities among the rocks. Both male and female fashion the nest from sticks, large laminarian stalks and other seaweeds, and line it with grass. The clutch of usually three pale blue eggs must be kept warm. Feathers are good heat insulators and so most birds have a bare area on their underside to help them incubate the eggs. This brood patch allows the eggs to gain heat directly from the warm skin. Shags and cormorants lack this brood patch and, instead, cover the eggs with their large webbed feet.

When young birds hatch, after about a month, they are ungainly looking creatures. For the following 50 days or more their parents run a shuttle service bringing them a regular supply of fish. Returning low and fast over the water, an adult rises steeply as it approaches the cliff, and loses speed before landing in a flurry with a loud flapping of its wings. The nestlings peck impatiently at the parent's bill until it regurgitates its catch. Then they jostle each other for the opportunity to lunge into the adult's gape, and push their beaks down into its gullet. As soon as one has emerged to swallow its meal, the next young makes its move. Once fed they settle back into the nest where they may be brooded by one of the adult birds if the weather is cold. On a fine summer's day, the opposite problem arises. Sheltered from the prevailing winds, the nest receives heat reflected from the surrounding white guano-covered rocks and the temperature soars. Any birds old enough to fly and adults not tending young return to the sea. Those which are stuck at the nest pant by sitting with open bill and flapping the throat to create a cooling movement of air.

Birds such as these with a long breeding season are vulnerable to disturbance in easily accessible sites. As this colony demonstrates, however, nesting birds do not necessarily require peace and quiet. There can be few other bird sanctuaries in the world that owe their seclusion to being aimed at by powerful guns. The shags and cormorants on the Mewstone continue to breed successfully, apparently unaffected by the fire from the opposite shore. Perhaps this is because, as far as is known, their island retreat has never been hit.

Travelling east along the south coast, the character of the country changes and with it the nature of the land. Startlingly chalk-white undulating cliffs sweep in a gentle curve to form Worbarrow Bay. Set against a bright blue sea, this is part of the magnificent shoreline of the Lulworth firing ranges in Dorset. From the remains of a fossilised forest, the cliffs rise to dominate a view backed by majestic chalk ridges clad in short grass. Further inland lies a huge heathland, some dry and some wet peat bog.

The Lulworth ranges enclose and preserve a rich and varied scene that has changed little in the latter half of this century. It is now a unique area for wildlife having been protected from the ravages of human housing developments, pesticides and pollution. Stretching over 10 kilometres along the shore and covering over 2800 hectares of ground, it contains three sites of special scientific interest. The ranges also form part of the Purbeck Heritage coast, which is internationally recognised as being of outstanding importance for wildlife, ranking alongside such areas as the French Camargue and the German Lune Heath.

The nature of Lulworth owes its continued survival to a revolutionary weapon of warfare. The invention of the armoured tank during the First World War led to the foundation of the Tank Corps and the need for a firing range. The first land at Lulworth was acquired in 1917 and in the following year gunners started training on the Bindon range. Further areas, including Heath range and Tyneham valley, were added during the Second World War. Today the Lulworth ranges are home to the Royal Armoured Corps Gunnery School. The latest armoured vehicles, including the Warrior and Challenger tanks, demand large areas in which to manoeuvre. Each year about 70 000 armour-piercing, high explosive and phosphorous smoke shells are fired. Some do not explode but ricochet and land anywhere on the range or in the sea. Public access is, therefore, severely limited, and there are only a few footpaths and tracks, mainly bordered by substantial fences and warning signs. Before opening these paths to the

DANGER
KEEP OUT
UNEXPLODED
SHELLS

The Lulworth ranges are used by the Royal Armoured Corps Gunnery School and public access is very restricted. The ranges include large areas of heath, chalk hill and grasslands (*main picture*) and the beautiful coastline of Worbarrow Bay (*bottom right*).

public, all routes are searched for unexploded shells. Yet incredibly, despite the crackle of small arms and the thunder of 120mm weapons, the ranges team with wildlife.

Although extensive areas have been planted with pine and parts have been badly churned by the passage of tanks, the heathland provides a refuge for some extraordinary creatures. In Britain the Dartford warbler is mainly confined to lowland heaths, preferring areas of mature heather and scattered tall gorse growth. While other warblers migrate, the Dartford remains to face the winter weather and harsh years take a severe toll. In the last century it was to be found across southern England, from Cornwall to Suffolk. Today it has the dubious honour of being one of the country's rarest breeding birds and the Dorset and Hampshire heaths are its last tenuous hold.

The heathland part of the ranges also supports many endangered species, such as the sand lizard, the smooth snake and the natterjack toad. Some 21 species of dragonflies and damselflies inhabit the flooded craters, streams, pools and the wet ditches flanking tank tracks, while grasshoppers and crickets abound. A few wading birds breed in these wet areas each year, including redshank, curlew and snipe, while the greenshank breeds in the Arctic but returns by late June. Another uncommon breeding bird, the nightjar, keeps mainly to drier parts of the heath and fringing pines. Here turtle doves can be heard, and a hobby may be seen chasing a large dragonfly.

Heaths are typically flat open lands with little elevation. However, the ridge road running along part of this chalk spine is high enough to offer breathtaking views. Kestrels hover along the steep slopes at eye-level above the short sheep-cropped turf. For thousands of years, the heathland has remained unploughed and refreshingly unimproved, allowing a rich flora to thrive. All around is visible evidence of ancient habitation. Bronze Age barrows survive on the heath and ridges. Yet more impressive are the Iron Age hillforts with huge earth ramparts, one of the largest of which is cut into the contours of Bindon Hill. Excavations indicate that an early invasion force built this as a beach-head defence against local tribes attacking from inland.

As I walked eastwards along the coastal footpath the air was filled with the song of skylarks and the scent of wild herbs, and I felt the springy turf of chalk and limestone grasslands beneath my feet. From springtime onwards the flowers bloom in ever-changing colours. Rare orchids and gentians grow alongside the pale pinks of squinancywort and mauve scabious, the yellows of vetches and trefoils, cowslips and wild parsnip, and the delicate blue of harebells. The broad leaves and long flowering shoots of wild cabbage looked strangely out of place along the cliffs, but this plant is very much at home here and is now almost confined to the coastal grasslands of Dorset.

East of Worbarrow Bay, nestled between the ridges of Whiteway Hill and the seaward scarp of Gad cliffs, lies a valley that time seems to have forgotten. There can be few places in Britain as untouched by chemical sprays or artificial fertilisers as Tyneham. Ancient field strips are still in evidence and it is possible that large areas were last cultivated some 1500 years ago. However, Tyneham is mentioned in the Domesday Book and a settlement continued to exist there until the Second World War. During this time, the farming practised by the rural community changed little. Then in 1943, the nearby Gunnery School required more land to cope with the increasing range of new weapons. The army requisitioned this valley, gaining over 2000 hectares and evicting many families within a month. It was understood at the time that the community would one day return, but the unexploded shells, which still lie embedded in the ground, made that impossible.

Today, abandoned buildings of the landed gentry and humbler dwellings of farm workers stand in varying states of dereliction. Some have lost roofs and upper storeys, while others have been reduced to bare shells. The garden flowers which still bloom below the staring empty windows are relics of the days when nature was kept at bay. Now ivy clambers up the stone walls and a tangle of plants guards each door. Lichens grow in profusion in the unpolluted air, both on the walls and especially on the trees. For these plants alone, Tyneham is of regional importance. The village centre is being refurbished and is open to the public on non-firing days. Repointed stonework and new roofing have provided a visitor centre and preserved the church. However, the real treasures of the valley lie outside the village, beyond the barbed wire.

In the cool of dawn there is an abundance of rabbits, and the coarse matted grass is alive with voles and shrews. These creatures attract the predatory foxes and badgers, stoats and weasels, hovering kestrels, and the mewing buzzards which wheel effortlessly overhead. Green and great spotted woodpeckers hammer at the trees, while in the half light of morning and dusk a barn owls may be seen but seldom heard.

A walk down through the valley away from the public path, which can only be done with special permission, reveals rough and unkempt ground bursting with a rich plant life. The grasslands of medieval England must have looked much like this, before modern farming methods excluded so many weeds and wild flowers. After years of neglect, the hedgerows have lost their layered look and appear more like woodland strips with mature trees. There is dense scrub of

The chalk grasslands are rich in wild flowers and insect life. The green bush cricket (*below left*) is common, while the Lulworth skipper butterfly (*below right*) is only found along this stretch of coast in Britain. The harebell (*bottom*), bird's foot trefoil (*opposite, inset*) and bee orchid (*opposite, main picture*) are all found on the Lulworth ranges.

blackthorn where brambles climb high, and in other areas the gorse has closed ranks. Many trees are reclining with age and fallen trunks are slowly being submerged beneath the rising rampant growth.

Some of the most prominent features of the grasslands are created by one of its smallest creatures, the yellow field ant. Mounds lie scattered in a random pattern across the slopes right up to the edge of the cliffs. Within each hillock a honeycomb of tunnels and chambers is home to perhaps over 20 000 ants. These industrious creatures build a mound gradually by moving soil a particle at a time, avoiding large stones and evicting smaller ones. The shape of the mound is generally not even, for the south-easterly side is angled to catch the warming rays of the early morning sun. The mounds often develop a flora quite distinct from that of the surrounding land as fine grasses and small flowering plants take root in the sifted soil. Many of the ant nests may be more than a century old and some are now quite substantial in size. Each is a breeding centre for a colony, and from it radiates a network of passages, spreading out into the turf beyond.

In each square metre of the grassy sward around the ants' home, there are up to 30 different species of plants. This variety is typical of chalk and limestone country, which has a shallow but humus-rich soil. It is relatively low in a number of nutrients, such as nitrogen, phosphorus, potassium and iron. However, it has good supplies of calcium as is shown by the abundance of snails which need calcium to build their shells. Such soil favours small, slow-growing plants.

Amongst the odd twisted metal remains of shell cases and the occasional rusting hulks used as targets, the ragged grasslands are alive with butterflies. In the absence of the insecticidal warfare waged by modern agriculture, marbled whites, meadow browns, gatekeepers and common blues dance in the sun. Over 30 species of butterfly and more than 120 moths have so far been identified on this range, as well as 353 beetles and 67 different spiders.

The number of butterflies is determined partly by the availability of their food plants. The caterpillar of the common blue feeds mainly on the leaves of the bird's foot trefoil, which thrives in chalk grasslands. Two other blue butterflies, the adonis and chalkhill blue, require not only food but also the presence of ants to survive.

These butterflies are restricted to the downland slopes of southern England where they fly during late summer. The female chalkhill blue lays her eggs singly on the stems and leaves of horseshoe vetch and other plants in August. These hatch the following April, and the green caterpillars, little more than 7 millimetres in length, begin to feed on the leaves of the vetch.

Like the larvae of other blue butterflies, the caterpillars secrete a sugary liquid called honeydew which is rich in amino acids and highly attractive to ants. Tiny glands covering the body help to give the larva a sweet coating. A larger gland near the tail secretes droplets of honeydew and the larva disperses these with the aid of two brush-like structures which periodically protrude from slits in its skin. Any yellow field ants in the vicinity soon swarm over the caterpillar and drink its secretions. It is common to find 20 or more ants on a single caterpillar, after it has emerged in early morning to feed.

This is a symbiotic relationship in which the ants gain honeydew and the caterpillar gains protection. The ants constantly tend the caterpillar and may carry it to a plant nearer their nest. At night, when the caterpillar descends to the ground, the ants remain close by and sometimes bury it beneath the soil to keep it safe from predators. They also keep at bay the large number of parasitic insects which seek out larvae in which to lay their eggs. As caterpillars grow they periodically shed their skins and for the following few days are very vulnerable. It is perhaps during these periods that the protection afforded by the ants is most beneficial.

After 10 weeks of growth, the chalkhill blue caterpillar pupates just under the soil surface. Even at this stage it continues to secrete some honeydew, and the ants remain in attendance. The following month it emerges into the grassland sun and climbs a stem. There its crumpled wings slowly unfurl, stiffen and dry. Only then does it leave the protection of the ants swarming below, and flutter up into the air.

Most of the butterflies and moths found on these ranges are easily distinguished but there is one insect that at first glance could be either. Its plain brown wings are half folded over its back when at rest in typical moth fashion. However, it flies by day and its antennae are club-shaped like a butterfly's rather than feathery, like a moth's. In fact, the Lulworth skipper is a butterfly and its tiny wings are actually a dusky gold colour. It comes from a widespread family, but this species is rarely found elsewhere in the world. In Britain it is restricted to the coastal hills of Dorset, extending west just into Devon. The Lulworth skipper feeds from wild flowers, particularly marjoram and thistles, while its tiny caterpillars consume the leaves of the heath false-brome, also known as tor grass. Clumps of this grass reaching over a metre in height are an attractive feature of the range.

The Lulworth skipper lays its eggs in rows in tor grass sheaths during July and August. The young caterpillars hatch after about three weeks but do not attempt to feed. Instead each constructs a silken shelter inside the sheath of grass, and remains within it throughout the winter. The larva emerges in April and feeds on the tender new growth of the grass at night, staying hidden in a

The village of Tyneham lies, for the most part, in ruins. But the villagers' loss is the wildlife's gain – the surrounding country is perhaps one of the last vestiges of how much of old England once looked.

folded blade by day. After three weeks of pupation, the butterfly emerges and sets off across the hills of the coast in search of nectar-rich flowers and a mate.

In past centuries, countless flocks of sheep tended by generations of farming folk kept the turf of the valley trimmed and the invasive scrub at bay. Today there are far fewer sheep grazing the pastures. If it were not for the rabbits introduced by the Normans in the twelfth century, the grasslands would have reverted to a wild tangled hawthorn scrub and this, in turn, would have given way to mature woodland. Over the last few decades, numbers have been reduced by the periodic return of the myxomatosis virus and some scrub has returned. This is a welcome feature, especially for birds.

At dusk a shrill melodious call from the scrub accompanies the descending dark. The drab brown plumage of the bird producing this virtuoso performance is seldom seen. Nightingales are shy, even by warbler standards, preferring to hide in dense thicket rather than stand out and sing. On arrival from their African winter quarters in late spring, the males sing to establish a territory and later, when the females have come, to attract a mate. By early summer they can be heard singing during the day as well as at night. They feed in daylight on earthworms, spiders, ground-living insects and berries. Nightingales conceal their nests as carefully as themselves, building close to the ground in thick undergrowth. Over much of southern Britain tidy farmland has reduced the scrub required by these birds, and the number of nightingales has dwindled. Only in surroundings such as at Tyneham can they continue to survive.

The area covered by the Lulworth ranges, particularly the Tyneham valley, is one of the few places in the country where three different deer species are found living close together. The smallest of these, the roe deer, has inhabited Dorset since prehistoric times. It is most often seen at dusk when it emerges from its daylight cover to feed on grass and browse among the brambles. In summer the leaves of broad-leafed trees, such as ash, hazel and oak, are also important sources of food. The deer may linger in the open for a few hours after dawn, alert for danger. If left undisturbed, roe may remain away from cover throughout the day, as they frequently do on the more remote parts of the range.

Unlike the sika and fallow deer with which they share this valley, the roe are not particularly social animals. Some may be solitary while others stay in small family groups often containing a male, female and one or two young. During the winter some of these groups come together to form loose herds. Unusually for deer, it is at this time of the year that the bucks grow their antlers. These have two sharp tines and are small in comparison with the spread of sika and fallow deer, seldom reaching more than 30 centimetres in length.

The roe buck establishes a territory in spring and differs from other deer in maintaining a stand for many months. In the process of stripping their antlers of skin, and later marking the boundaries of their declared ground, they can cause considerable damage to trees. They do this by fraying saplings, often stripping the bark and breaking the branches. In commercial plantations it is this behaviour that renders their stay unwelcome. The roe rutting season is earlier than most other deer, in July and August. Other bucks are challenged and fights are not uncommon with sometimes fatal results. During rutting bucks, does and young make well-trodden rings round a tree or stump, but the reason for this is not understood.

Fallow deer, although present, are not common on the range and are less likely to be seen than the introduced sika. This distant relative of the larger indigenous red deer is native to Japan and the far east. It was introduced at various times into feral herds scattered across the country, and is now naturalised and thriving. Like red deer, sika are grazing animals rather than browsers, feeding principally on grasses and sedges. Other important winter foods include ivy, holly, heather and young conifers, and sika are also known to eat chestnuts, acorns and some fungi. They are most active at dawn and dusk, moving out of the scrub and woodland to graze during the night and returning to cover at first light.

From four years of age the handsome stags carry up to eight points on their antlers, while older males may occasionally grow up to eleven.

Sika are sociable animals, living for much of the year in sexually segregated herds. After the rut in November they come together to form large mixed herds and in the following spring, the herds re-group. The stags cast and regrow their antlers while the hinds and young remain together. In both groups there is a pecking order with a dominant stag and hind rising through the ranks.

In the autumn, the clash of antlers may be the only sound to be heard through the mist enshrouding the valley at dawn. When the red flags are flying, no one walks this range and the wildlife is left in seclusion. The openness of the Dartmoor range, the limited access around the naval guns on the coast and the securely closed gates and fencing of Tyneham valley provide progressively safer havens. Protected, yet carefully managed, such wild areas owe their existence to the need for the armed services to train. The increasing interest shown by the Ministry of Defence in the wildlife of the ranges is helping to ensure that their rich diversity of life continues to thrive. It is ironic that some of our most beautiful countryside survives only because people are restricted by the projectiles whistling overhead and the unexploded shells embedded in the ground.

CHAPTER 6

Wild Game

The medieval castle of Powderham in Devon floated in a sea of mist at daybreak. Beneath the battlements a fallow deer buck threw back its fine head and bellowed a deep groaning roar. Beyond, where the stout trunks of aged oaks stood tall in the planted parkland, a cock pheasant strutted resplendent in its winter plumage. The scene could have been set at any time over the past 600 years, yet it was not a natural one. All the creatures in view belonged to a select group of animals that have been labelled game. In pursuit of such quarry, vast areas of Britain were left wild or managed in a way that maintained the number of game to the detriment of some less valued species and the benefit of others. Today, many of the great estates of Britain are among the largest privately owned reserves of wildlife in the country.

To most people, the term game means all those animals which have traditionally been hunted for food. However, the legal definition of game includes mainly the creatures prized by the nobility. So, for example, roebuck, partridge, hare and sea trout are counted as game, while rabbit, woodpigeon and teal are not. Some birds, such as the large woodland grouse, the capercaillie, were extinct by 1831 in Britain when the Game Act reached the statute books and so are not included.

The capercaillie has subsequently been reintroduced and is today found in many northern forests.

In contrast, the bustard was included in the Game Act and is now extinct in Britain. There are many other anomalies. Snipe and woodcock can be shot as game, yet their close season is protected by the Countryside and Wildlife Act. A game licence is required to shoot snipe but not ducks and geese. Game laws vary in England, Scotland and Ireland, with deer being included by some and not by others.

The preservation of game has a tradition of the highest order in Britain. Monarchs such as King Canute and Malcolm II of Scotland were the first to declare protection for deer and salmon. More formal legislation followed with the arrival of the Normans and their passion for hunting. William I established the first forest laws and set aside large areas of land for the hunt. The first reference to game in English law seems to appear in 1389, during the reign of Richard II. Such laws were based on the right of kings and queens to lay claim to all game. They were designed to protect the animals hunted by the nobility and defined the social status and property-owning qualifications necessary for anyone wishing to hunt 'gentlemen's game'. There were no restrictions on the sons of a Baron or Knight, or someone higher in the social scale. For those lower down, the punishments for breaking the law were harsh and barbaric, even by the standards of the day. While sentences of death and mutilation have disappeared along with the man traps used against poachers, the involvement of the Crown and the hunters' financial status are reflected in modern law. The right to kill or take game is still conferred by the Crown although this is now granted upon purchase of a game licence rather than by royal prerogative.

In the years following the Norman invasion, the pursuit of game moved outside the royal forests. This was a period of feudal unrest, and loyalties to a particular overlord were repaid with the endowment of a title and land. Many of the great estates surviving today can trace their roots back hundreds of years, some to Norman times. Powderham Castle, set alongside the magnificent Exe estuary, has been the seat of the Courtenay family for more than 600 years. Now possessing the title the Earl of Devon, the family can trace its history back to Norman times and a courtier who came to England in 1152 with Eleanor of Aquitaine, the wife of Henry II. When a fortified manor house was first built at Powderham in 1390, its land included a substantial part of the county of Devon.

Tree-planted parklands and landscaped grounds are a feature of these great houses. Not far from the Exe estuary lies the equally impressive house of Ugbrook, with neat sheep-trimmed grass stretching down to a series of lakes. Following the Teign valley further inland, the large mature trees at Canonteign are a reminder of the age of these estates. Here, the beauty of the scenery is enhanced by the highest waterfall in England which tumbles over a steep rock face. Despite the apparent permanence of this spectacular feature, it is relatively modern. The fall was created in the last century by diverting a stream and channelling it over a precipice. For all its seeming naturalness, the wildlife of these large estates has also been extensively managed. This has had far-reaching consequences, transforming the species found and their abundance. When these estates were first created, their nature and the methods of hunting employed were very different.

The hunting of game birds was widespread long before the invention of firearms. The use of a bow and arrow for felling flying birds was rarely if ever entertained, and snaring and trapping were used to little effect. Instead, people harnessed the talents of the natural predators, hawks and falcons. Falconry has an ancient origin, extending back certainly to Saxon times and probably long before. Medieval men took a passionate interest in their birds, and developed falconry into an elaborate art involving ceremonies, rules and restrictions. The type of hawk a person was permitted to own depended on their rank and social standing. The peregrine, gyrfalcon and goshawk were reserved for the gentry, while those of humbler origin were allowed to carry the kestrel and sparrowhawk. The latter bird became particularly associated with the clergy, although bishops, who were classified as noblemen, had a greater choice.

In the Middle Ages considerable expense was lavished on birds of prey. Good birds could change hands literally for a King's ransom: a Crusader prince was rescued from the Saracens on payment of twelve Greenland falcons. This transaction gives some idea of the value of the international trade which developed around falconry. By Tudor times, hawking had become so popular that Henry VII and his successor introduced stringent laws to protect the birds and their nests. Eventually the enthusiasm for falconry started to lessen due as much to a change in fashion and the lack of interest of the Hanoverian kings, as to the development of the gun. Its decline was helped by the enclosure of open lands, the draining of fens, the gradual destruction of forests and, finally, the invention of shot. A deadly spread of lead pellets dramatically increased the chances of hitting a flying target.

Guns were probably fired at birds in fifteenth-century Europe but at first they would have made little impact on the number killed. In 1533, when wildfowl were being shot in Norfolk with the new wheel-lock gun, falconry was still at its height. Then early in the seventeenth century the flintlock was developed, and by the end of the century guns were in general use for hunting.

Although we may not realise it, the seemingly 'natural' surroundings of Powderham Castle (*below, main picture*) and its folly (*inset*) are as much a result of man's activity as the buildings themselves. Even spectacular features such as the highest waterfall in England, at Canonteign (*opposite*), are an example of landscaping on a grand scale.

Over the following centuries the refinement of the breech-loading shotgun, coupled with an expanding human population, radically altered the hunt. Greater firepower and a new mobility gave access to wilder country, and driven game shoots began.

The nature of Britain has seen great changes since Norman times, but none so profound and far-reaching as those of the last two centuries. Animals and plants have become extinct while others have been introduced. Many consider that today Britain's wildlife is largely composed of those species which people have allowed to survive. Those animals which were exploited as a source of food were maintained at the expense of their natural predators.

By the beginning of the 1800s, many sporting estates had game keepers. Charged with rearing and protecting large numbers of game birds, they viewed natural predators as vermin, and shot, trapped and poisoned them on a huge scale. The consequences for many wild species were catastrophic and some birds of prey were virtually wiped out. A demand for skins added to the pressures on wildlife, as the trade in taxidermy grew to meet the Victorian passion for collecting. Cases of stuffed birds adorned many houses of the age, and some people became avid collectors of eggs, amassing hundreds in closed drawers.

It was once common to see weasels and stoats hanging in line from the keeper's gibbet. In reality the small fast-moving weasels are ruthless hunters of rodents, following mice and voles through their tunnels deep underground. They will readily tackle rats, and only a tiny part of their diet is made up of small birds and their eggs. Stoats are more of a problem for game rearers because these mammals will take game birds and poultry. If they find penned birds, they will occasionally kill far in excess of their needs. However, it is thought that stoats only prey on game during the short period of breeding. Throughout the rest of the year they offset this damage by killing rats, mice and voles, while rabbits form a principal part of their diet.

One bird which was accused of taking game chicks even provoked a national debate. The little owl was introduced to various parts of the country during the latter half of the nineteenth century, and had mixed success at first. Further releases strengthened its numbers and, as the population grew, so did the controversy. In 1937 the bird became the subject of the first enquiry organised by the British Trust for Ornithology. Their findings vindicated the little owl. The smallest of the five species of owl found in Britain, it hunts as much by day as by night. While it does take some mammals and small birds, particularly starlings and sparrows, a large proportion of its food is made up of invertebrates, such as worms, beetles, slugs and snails.

Birds of prey, especially buzzards and tawny owls, used to be persecuted by gamekeepers. Both are known to take the occasional young game bird, but they mainly prey on rodents and, in the case of the buzzard, rabbits – which more than compensates the keeper's loss. Rooks sometimes display a partiality for other birds' eggs and young and this has been their undoing in some areas. However, rooks are generally considered useful by farmers because they feast in the fields on the larvae of root-eating insects. The closely related crows and magpies, on the other hand, are generally shot on sight.

Today most estates concentrate on the control of foxes, magpies and crows, which are considered the main threats to successful game rearing. Electric fencing and tunnel traps for mink, stoats and rats all help to reduce the loss of young game birds. Wildlife is legally protected in Britain now. However, the law cannot prevent a minority of keepers clinging to the misguided beliefs and prejudices of their forbears and wantonly killing predators.

The captive breeding of pheasants and partridges is undertaken on a huge scale by the larger estates. Specialist breeders run game farms which supply keepers with day-old chicks to be reared in a series of pens. In the months following the winter shooting season, gamekeepers also catch many hens and sufficient cock birds to form a reservoir for a captive breeding colony. In the past broody hens and bantams served as foster mothers, hatching and rearing young pheasant and partridge chicks. Today, the eggs are hatched in the carefully controlled environment of incubators. Kept at a constant temperature and humidity, and turned regularly by machines, great numbers of the eggs produce young.

The incubator-hatched chicks' path to freedom lies through a succession of enclosures. Brooding pens heated by lamps are followed by rain-protected shelters covering short grass, and then larger runs mainly open to the elements. The final stage, the releasing pen, is usually secreted in a quiet copse where trees offer shelter and a safe retreat. Special openings in the wire allow the birds which have flown to return for food when necessary. On some estates, several thousand birds are released in a single season. From the carefully nurtured safety of their upbringing they are now out on their own. For many, the freedom will be short-lived. At most, around 40 per cent of those released are ever likely to be shot but the majority of bags on well-stocked shoots are made up of first-year birds. Of the remainder, some fall to predators or the vagaries of the British climate. Poaching, accidental injury and disease also take their toll. The birds which elude the guns and the other hazards may live for several years, adapting to and learning about the countryside in which they now live. Some settle on safe ground where guns seldom go. Others are not easily flushed by beaters and so live to see another

In the past much of Britain's wildlife was persecuted in the name of game protection. Magpies (*below right*) are a genuine menace, but buzzards (*below left*) feed more on small mammals and even worms. Sparrowhawks (*opposite top*) take mainly small birds in flight and the little owl (*opposite bottom*) feeds almost exclusively on beetles and worms.

shooting season. The cocks, especially, become wily by the end of the year and learn to double back so that only a clever keeper, who reverses the direction of the last beats, will flush them out. The survivors, particularly the female pheasants, may add to the wild breeding stock.

Although the majority of private estates in Britain are only a fraction of their former size, the rearing of game birds has intensified. Each year more than 10 million pheasants and over a million partridges are released into the wild. The cost of breeding and keepering runs into hundreds of millions of pounds. Yet despite all the care and money lavished on the quarry, the numbers of Britain's game are on the decline. In the 20 years between 1965 and 1985 the number of pheasants released annually doubled. The number of birds shot did not rise nearly as much, yet many more were dying before reaching adulthood.

Since the 1920s, for example, the population of the native grey partridge has crashed by 95 per cent. In the early 1960s brown hares could be seen in large numbers, flushed from fields during harvesting. Now their numbers have declined dramatically and they are absent from many former haunts. It seems to be mainly farmland game species such as these which are suffering a downward trend and this has been brought about largely by changes in practice. Traditional farming methods have given way to a deluge of agrochemicals, the destruction of hedgerows and a general tidying up of the land. Yet in forest plantations deer are on the increase, as, in some areas, are woodcock.

Both numerically and economically, the most important game bird in Britain is undoubtedly the pheasant. It is also the best known and is easily recognised by most people as it struts about in its gaudy iridescent plumage. Yet the pheasant is not native to Britain but an exotic immigrant. According to ancient legend, Jason and the returning Argonauts first brought the pheasant to Europe from the valley of the River Phasis. Situated in the Colchis region of the Caucasus, the valley lies in an area now known as the Soviet Republic of Georgia. This story of the pheasant's origin, referred to in ancient writings and reinforced by early naturalists such as Pliny, has been perpetuated in its scientific name, *Phasianus colchicus.*

The pheasant is generally thought to have been introduced into Britain by the Romans, who recorded details on rearing and recipes for cooking these highly prized birds. They do not seem to have been included in Roman dinners when Julius Caesar's troops first invaded Britain, but may have appeared in the later stages of occupation. The only evidence that the Romans imported pheasants comes from a few remains found in excavations at Corbridge in Northumberland. The pheasant probably began its life in Britain as a farmyard fowl, kept and carefully reared by the wealthier households. Such a valuable bird, destined for a culinary dish, is unlikely to have been allowed to roam freely and few if any became established in the wild.

During the Dark Ages which followed the Roman withdrawal, records became obscure and with them the fate of the pheasant. The next evidence of pheasants being introduced dates from the year 1059, some six centuries after the last Roman legions had left Britain. The first large-scale importations probably did not occur until the arrival of the Normans towards the end of the eleventh century.

By the latter half of the sixteenth century, pheasants had become widespread across England. The birds were introduced to other parts of Britain, but did not become common in Wales until the middle of the last century.

That the pheasant managed not only to survive but to breed successfuly in the wild in Britain may appear surprising for it was an exotic living in an alien environment. The birds also had to adapt to major changes in the countryside brought about by deforestation, the agricultural revolution and the division of land following the Enclosure Acts, which created more hedgerow cover. However, all of these suited the pheasant and the birds thrived.

The pheasant is native to an area extending from the Caucasus and Caspian eastwards through central Siberia to Burma and China. The birds are absent from northern Scandinavia, Portugal and western Spain and occur elsewhere in Europe only as introductions. The original stock introduced from the Caucasus became known as the old English pheasant. From 1785, large numbers of birds from China were released. These had a characteristic white collar which gave rise to the ring-necked or Chinese pheasant. The Japanese pheasant, brought in in 1840, was renowned for its handsome appearance, size and strong flight, and had a reputation for not straying far. The Mongolian pheasant was released in Britain in the early nineteenth century. All these races have freely interbred producing a wide variation in colour and characteristics. The white neck ring remains a common feature among cock birds, distinguishing them from the many other bright plumaged varieties of ornamental pheasants, which are bred mainly for their striking colours.

The pheasant inhabits grasslands with a good scattered cover of shrubs and trees. In its native lands it is found along the margins of rivers, foraging around reed beds. Only in East Anglia do British pheasants frequent such places but throughout the country the birds prefer well-watered land. That pheasants are at home around wetlands is shown by the readiness with which they take to water, and they swim surprisingly well. Trees are another important element of the pheasant's habitat, providing shelter and a safe roost clear of the ground. For this

Wild cock pheasants (*below*) establish a territory into which many hens may stray. The nest (*opposite*) is usually a scrape under dense vegetation. After hatching, the chicks follow their mother around for up to two weeks and indulge in dust-bathing.

reason, they are absent from the highest ground, and moors and open areas support few, while well-wooded farmland, parks and large estates contain the greatest populations. They thrive especially where thick cover lies adjacent to fields of light soil where the birds can feed. Their numbers are kept high in many areas by an annual influx of releases. Away from game reserves the density of pheasants is much lower. However, wild populations do maintain their numbers in some regions. Around 30 pairs live on Brownsea Island off Poole, where they have survived for over 40 years with no game management at all.

The cock birds are spectacular as they emerge from cover, especially early or late in the day when a red-tinged sun makes their colours glow. Although their hue is variable, they are usually mainly copper coloured with a glossy green head and scarlet wattles surrounding the eyes. Two short ear tufts of fine feathers set off the exotic head. The tail is no less attractive, and the two central tail feathers can grow to a considerable length, reaching about 46 centimetres in most males and 61 centimetres in the oldest birds.

The hen pheasant is more subdued in colour, and her mottled brown feathers merge well with her surroundings, especially when she is nesting in undergrowth. A cock establishes a territory which may cover an area the size of two football fields, while the hens move around in groups. A single hen may wander over an area overlapping the territories of four or more cocks. Pairs usually only remain together for a short period. Although there are records of cock birds assisting with incubation and attempting to brood, the males generally return after mating to guard their territory and court more mates.

The female pheasant often makes a nest by scraping a hollow in dry ground under the cover of thick undergrowth, such as brambles, and lining it with leaves and grass. Occasionally she will nest in haystacks or beneath cut brushwood, and may even take over the disused nest of another species in a tree. A hen usually lays between 7 and 15 pale olive-brown eggs and can lay as many as 20. If there are more in a nest, it probably holds two clutches. Laying takes place at any time from March to September but most eggs are laid from April to June.

The hen incubates the eggs, relying on her camouflage to avoid detection. She may also adopt another technique, which is used by grouse. Research has shown that if a sitting grouse is approached by a dog or fox, she visibly shrinks on to the nest, her heart rate falls dramatically and the body processes slow down. In this state, any scent she normally produces is greatly reduced. This helps her to escape the notice of predators, such as foxes, which rely heavily on their sense of smell to find prey. If a predator comes too close, her heart rate leaps a hundredfold in less than a second and she erupts into the air.

When a hen pheasant leaves her nest to feed she often covers her clutch with leaves. There are many sharp-eyed predators around and unconcealed eggs will be quickly snatched by a magpie or crow. Up to 27 days after laying the attractive, cryptically marked chicks start to hatch. The well-developed young dry out and are on their feet within a few hours. Soon they all leave the nest, following their mother to find food, and are fully fledged within 12 to 14 days. At first, the chicks rest under the protective shelter of their mother's wings, but as they grow older they become more independent. Pheasants are not good at defending their young and several may fall to predators. Although the birds generally rear only one brood each year, they may nest again following disaster.

Pheasants are shy, wary birds, even when semi-domesticated. If caught in the open they will quickly scurry to the nearest cover or, if already partly concealed, they will crouch until danger passes. They appear loathe to fly and prefer to run quickly ahead of beaters and their dogs. The faster they run, the higher the tail is held. When compelled to fly they do so with explosive force, and can lift vertically if necessary to clear surrounding trees. During their fast and direct ascent, the short rounded wings whirr noisily. Once sufficient height has been gained, the pheasant glides silently on down-curved wings and drops back into cover.

The pheasant is most active at dawn and dusk. It is possible to approach feeding pheasants quite closely in a vehicle, a fact which is often their undoing. They frequently forage alongside roads and country lanes, and road casualties are common. In reply to a distant call, the cock birds raise their heads and utter a strident crow, usually followed by a brief whirr of wing flapping. They also respond to loud noises, such as the sound of a gun, a quarry blast, thunder and even the sonic boom left in Concorde's wake.

During fine days pheasant may indulge in one of their favourite pursuits, dust bathing. A well-used spot becomes hollowed out as the birds scratch, frantically roll and then fluff out their feathers. While watching a hen begin this daily ritual, I was amused to see the chicks imitating her and covering themselves liberally with dust. Such baths presumably help in some way to keep the birds' feathers in good condition. Whatever the reason, most game birds spend a good part of any fine day rolling around in dry soil.

Today, pheasants are common and make up 85 per cent of the annual bag of game birds in the lowlands of Britain. Yet it is only through the efforts of people over nearly 1000 years that the pheasant survives here at all. The rearing of pheasant has been likened by some to the fattening of cattle and sheep, but the economics of it are much more daunting. A single bird can cost more than £12 to rear and release. In the past, it was said of pheasant shoots, 'Up goes a guinea,

Waterways (*below*) and flood-filled ditches attract large numbers of wildfowl in winter. *Opposite top* Where beans are used as pheasant feed and left to dry in the field, wild flowers erupt – ox-eye daisies and corn marigolds. *Opposite bottom* Headlands planted with different crops provide additional cover for game birds.

bang goes tuppence and down comes half-a-crown'. While inflation and changes in currency have altered the amounts, the relative costs remain the same. Those who wish to take part in the larger shoots must be prepared to pay handsomely for it.

Far smaller than the introduced pheasant and sought after with a similar passion, is the native grey partridge. Until the outbreak of the First World War, this bird held the premier place on shooting estates. Many keepers went to war and, like so many young men of the time, did not return. The subsequent shortage of labour meant that many partridge shoots were poorly managed and the number of birds declined. A company which manufactured shotgun cartridges and had a near monopoly of the market experienced a dramatic slump in profits. As a result, it financed the Eley Game Advisory Service to investigate the birds. This later became the Game Conservancy, which is a research organisation funded almost entirely by voluntary subscription and sponsorship. Through the work of these and other bodies, the grey partridge is now one of the most intensively studied birds in Britain. Indeed, so much is known about these birds that they are considered by many to be a good candidate for an indicator species, measuring the general health of wildlife.

In autumn and early winter partridges live in small family groups, known as coveys. These usually consist of two or more older birds and a number of young. After a successful breeding season a covey may contain seven or eight offspring and their parents, while in a bad year it may include only three or four birds, most of them males. The females are particularly vulnerable during the incubation of their eggs, for if they are disturbed they will sit tight. Up to a quarter of them may be taken by foxes, stoats and the increasing populations of feral cats prowling far from urban sprawls, while in some areas mink account for a considerable number.

If a covey is disturbed the birds will squat at first, but if approached too closely they will erupt into the air like an exploding feather bomb. Grey partridges are among the most sedentary of birds and seldom fly far. Indeed, they spend the majority of their lives in just a few adjacent fields.

By midwinter the birds have begun to pair off, unless the weather is particularly bad. The grey partridge nests on the ground beneath the cover of a dense hedgerow with a good growth of grass flanking its roots. A well-drained place slightly raised on a hedge bank is a favoured nesting site. Even so, sudden squalls producing heavy downpours of rain destroy many partridge nests each year. The size of the clutch appears to vary with the age of the female, and usually totals 12 to 18 pale olive or buff eggs. Like the pheasant, a larger number is probably the result of two females laying in the same nest.

The eggs are laid on consecutive days, usually between 10 am and noon, and the 24-day incubation period begins when the last egg is laid. Most clutches are complete by the end of May so that the chicks hatch in June when the insect life on which they feed is at its peak. The grey partridge male is a devoted mate and remains close by. Although incubation is done by the hen alone, the male helps to tend the chicks. In the event of danger, both parents may feign injury to lure a predator away from the nest. Sometimes they defend their brood more aggressively and will even attack creatures as large as dogs. The chicks begin feeding within a few hours of hatching and can fly within a fortnight.

The grey partridge is found from northern Spain across central Europe into Asia. In Britain, it was once the most common game bird of the lowlands but populations have dwindled to an all-time low. While its decline in the 1920s was attributed to inadequate management of shoots, a further plummet in numbers during the 1960s indicated other problems. This was a period when persistent, highly toxic chemical insecticides were used extensively for the first time and these were blamed. However, more than 20 years later many of the early chemicals have been banned and the partridge populations have not recovered. It now appears that a combination of factors has led to its decline, including the availability of food, the weather, predation and changes in farming practice.

Large areas of the countryside are no longer suitable for partridges to survive in the wild. The tidying of land has reduced the number of birds, for the so-called marginal wastes are where partridge mainly forage. Fields are seldom left fallow and efficient modern machinery cleans the land, leaving little spilt grain. After the harvest many fields are burnt, and autumn ploughing has become the rule rather than the exception. This has reduced one of the partridge's staple foods, a species of sawfly larvae. However, spring ploughing is probably more damaging because it disturbs the birds when they are beginning to breed.

The recent farming trend towards increasing arable crops has resulted in a dramatic increase in field size. Cereal farmers especially consider that hedges are reservoirs for pests and diseases and so remove hedgerows or spray herbicides right up to the field edge. Although herbicides are generally not lethal to animal life, they kill many of the food plants that support the insects upon which the partridge chicks depend.

A microscopic analysis of the faecal products of young game birds has revealed their almost exclusive dependence on insects during the first few weeks of life. Caterpillars, other larvae, beetles and bugs provide a richer source of protein, and are more easily digested, than the plant material consumed by adult birds. Hedgerows and the field edges are where the greatest numbers of

The native grey partridge lays, on average, 12–18 eggs. All the eggs hatch within a couple of hours of each other and both parents protect the young. The red-legged partridge (*bottom*) was introduced to this country and, because of its better survival rate, is replacing the native variety of partridge – especially in the east of England.

insects survive on farmland. They also provide the preferred breeding sites for ground-nesting game birds.

Research has also indicated ways of reversing the decline. For example, it was discovered that by leaving a 6-metre wide strip around the margin of a field unsprayed, a spectacular survival rate for young birds was achieved. The increase in numbers was out of all proportion to the area set aside. Furthermore, the farmers saved expensive chemicals and there was no apparent loss of crop yield. Grey partridge and pheasant broods increased by more than half and survival rates more than doubled. The success of these species was accompanied by other bonuses. Songbirds abounded and butterflies trebled in number.

At present such practices are not widespread and on many estates people have given up shooting the few remaining grey partridges. Instead they have turned their attention and guns to the introduced red-legged partridge. This striking brown plumaged bird is easily distinguished from the smaller grey partridge by its black and white eye stripes, the rich chestnut barring on its grey flanks, and the lack of a horseshoe-shaped mark on its breast. It also has a red bill and, of course, red legs. The red-legged partridge is one of the few game species endemic to Europe alone. It is native to the south-west of the continent, inhabiting Spain, France, north-west Italy and the island of Corsica. Its range has now been increased by introductions. The first recorded import of the birds into Britain occurred in 1673. Other attempts at introduction followed until in 1790, the Marquis of Hertford in Suffolk brought in several thousand eggs from France. These were hatched and reared in captivity and then released to breed in the wild.

Despite suggestions to the contrary, there is little evidence that the red-legged partridge is in direct competition with our native bird. The red-legged prefers warmer, drier regions than the grey, as revealed by areas in which it has become established. It is concentrated in the central, southern and eastern parts of England, occurring only in isolated pockets further to the north and west. East Anglia offers the optimum conditions with low rainfall, light soils and intensive farming which opened up the countryside. The fortunes of this French introduction closely paralleled those of the grey partridge until the 1950s. Since then there has been a general increase in numbers and today the red-legged partridge's distribution is probably as wide as it has ever been. In some regions releases of other partridges, including the closely related chukar and rock partridges from south-east Europe, have resulted in hybrid birds.

The red-legged's greater success is due partly to its resilience and to aspects of its breeding behaviour. Both males and females play an active part in rearing the young. Uniquely among British birds, the female may lay a clutch of eggs in two nests, one for her and one for her mate. But the high number of eggs produced is offset by a greater loss. Unlike the grey, the red-legged partridge does not cover the eggs on leaving the nest and so many more are found and taken by predators. The eggs are also not laid on consecutive days and may be left for up to two days at a time. Incredibly, even eggs which have been left uncovered for weeks before being incubated still hatch successfully.

Many shooters consider the red-legged partridge to be inferior to the grey because it is even more reluctant to fly. Generally, it will run instead of sitting tight and wait to be flushed out. On wet clayey ground, the birds' feet may become so weighed down with caked mud that they cannot fly. Coveys are often large and when they do take to the air they scatter more widely than the grey.

While the pheasant, partridge and grouse are all sought after by shooters, the hare is the only mammal which has been hunted as game in Britain using a shotgun. Hunting hares has an ancient history extending back over thousands of years. Records of Egyptian and Mediterranean civilisations show that long ago the hare was pursued by specially bred dogs hunting by sight. In this country, the Celts and Saxons kept large gazehounds, the forerunners of today's greyhounds and deerhounds. Hare hunting with beagles, harriers and other hounds, which rely mainly on a sense of smell, became established here in Norman times. Over the last two centuries, the premier hunts have chased foxes, but medieval hunters gave pride of place to the hare.

The hare's importance throughout history has earned it a prominent role in folklore and legend. Witchcraft and sorcery, evils and the occult, have all laid sinister claim to the life and death of the animal. Greek and Roman writers on natural history, from Aristotle to Aelian, claimed that the hare could change its sex in alternate years. The belief that both male and female hares could give birth to young continued right up to the seventeenth century, while the tale that a witch could turn into a hare and then run away persisted into modern times.

The hare's native range extends from Europe as far as China, and it has been introduced to both North and South America, and even New Zealand and parts of Australia. In Britain, its strongholds are the dry arable lowlands of the east and central regions. Here its density may be three times higher than on traditional pasture land to the west of the country.

An elegant, fleet animal, the native brown hare cannot be confused with any other mammal in the country. It is twice the weight of a buck rabbit and its long legs give it a characteristic bounding gait quite unlike the rabbit's hop and scamper. It is an animal of the open field, relying on its speed to outdistance any

Below The brown hare is an elegant, long-legged creature with distinctive black tips to its ears. Hares live above ground and, contrary to popular belief about males boxing, their mad March antics are more often females resisting the attention of a male. The rabbit (*opposite*) is smaller than the hare and has shorter ears.

predator. The long black-tipped ears and the rich brown colour of the hare's end of year coat stand out against a field of green winter barley. The hare remains above ground throughout its life, resting during the day in a purpose-made scrape, called a form. From dusk to dawn it feeds on open ground, and for much of the year may be solitary. However, at the approach of spring the hare undergoes a distinct change of character.

In the pale light of dawn after a warm night, the mating antics, which have given rise to the proverbial mad March hare, can be seen. The animals combine high-speed chasing, great leaps and bounding with 'boxing matches'. Contrary to the beliefs of past generations of hare watchers, the fights are not usually between males. Most encounters involve a non-receptive female and the unwelcome advances of a male. In such matches the hares stand erect and spar using their front paws accompanied by flying fur and vigorous kicks.

It is possible that some of the mystique surrounding the hare comes from its ability, shared with rabbits, to absorb its embryos. This permits a pregnant hare to be mated and then conceive a second time before giving birth to the first young, but the survival value of this strategy is not fully understood. Hares can be prolific, with the females giving birth to three or four leverets at a time and producing up to four litters a year. After a six-week gestation, the young are born fully furred with their eyes open. If necessary, they can walk on their own within a few hours. The much less well-developed rabbit young are kept hidden in a burrow underground, but the hare adopts a different strategy. The leverets remain quiet and still, scattered in individual sheltered forms some way from where their mother is feeding. This has the advantage that if a form is found by a passing fox, only one leveret will be taken. The mother hare visits the young regularly and suckles each in turn. They are weaned and able to fend for themselves within a few weeks, but do not reach full size until they are about eight months old.

Once a very common animal of Britain's lowlands, the hare is now in decline. The problem was masked for a time by the decimation of the rabbit during the myxomatosis epidemic of 1954. Without rabbits to keep them in check, the grasslands grew providing more cover for hares. The predators which relied on rabbits also crashed and hare populations erupted. Since then the number of hares has diminished in line with many game birds.

Considering that the hare has been so passionately pursued by so many, it seems extraordinary that few people bothered to study it in detail, until quite recently. A few years of study have revealed that intensive farming is at least partly to blame for the decline. Hares thrive where there is a wide range of arable crops, and make far greater use than was previously thought of hedgerows and woods. They give fields used for pasture a wide berth until several days after the livestock have moved on. In some areas, it appears that large populations of hares are heavily predated by foxes, although foxes undoubtedly consume substantially more rabbits.

While the hare is a creature of farmland, many large country estates have encouraged and kept herds of deer. At present Britain is home to six species, with a combined population estimated at 750,000. Even by African standards, deer are big game, and this may seem a high number for such a small, crowded island. Yet few people have ever seen a deer outside a zoo or park. Despite hundreds of years of close association with people, deer remain timid. Always alert, shy and suspicious, they are among the most beautiful and elusive of species. Although there is evidence to suggest that the fallow was resident here long ago, only red and roe deer have been native to Britain since the last ice age. The Romans are credited with first importing the fallow, and large-scale releases date from Norman times. Over the last century sika, muntjac and Chinese water deer have also been introduced, mainly to private estates.

Deer use their well-developed senses to detect danger and rely on their speed and uncanny knack of disappearing into the smallest cover to evade predators. In the past, the numbers of native red and roe deer were kept down by wolves, bears and lynx. These large carnivores were removed by the growing human population and today the main threats are foxes, which only take the young, and people. From earliest times people have killed deer for food and after the Norman invasion deer became a focus for the formal hunt. Although people still hunt deer, the dearth of natural predators has meant that deer also have to be controlled by selective culling. Even so, deer populations are increasing against the trend of most other game species. It is possible that there are more deer today than in the time of Robin Hood, despite the massive loss of deciduous woodland that covered large tracts of the country in those far-off days.

Fallow deer are depicted at Powderham Castle in drawings dating from 1775, and they are thought to have been present long before this. Carefully managed and controlled, the deer nevertheless remain wild and can only be glimpsed at a distance by visitors. The fallow deer year could be said to begin with the birth of the young in June. When this event is imminent, a female seeks the seclusion of tall grass or bracken under trees, and there produces a single fawn or, rarely, twins. The mother carefully tends her young and licks it clean, while remaining on her feet, alert and watching for danger. Within a few hours, the fawn stands unsteadily on feet at first widely splayed. Once it has started suckling, its

The fallow is the most widespread and common deer in Britain and many can be found in parklands such as these at Powderham. Mature bucks grow a new set of antlers each year ready for the autumn rut and the young are born in May and June.

strength grows and the fawn is able to run within 24 hours. For the next ten days the young remains under cover, relying on its dappled colouring to keep it hidden among the spangled shade. About two weeks after birth, it joins its mother, and feeds with the rest of the herd. The young may continue to suckle for a further nine months or even a year, and it is not uncommon to find newborn and yearling fawn at foot.

By June the bucks have lost their splendid antlers, which in many areas disappear without trace. Where calcium is in short supply, the deer themselves may chew on the cast bone-like structures, reabsorbing the minerals invested in their formation. Other animals too will gnaw at antlers, including, after dark, the woodmouse. Antlers are solid and grow each year from two raised circular bones on the skull, known as pedicles. These are contained within a covering of skin and are well supplied with blood. Growth usually begins shortly after the old pair have been shed and can continue until late summer.

The size and form of the antlers depends on the buck's age and on the mineral richness of the area in which the deer feeds. The antlers of a year-old buck are seldom more than enlarged knobs. After three or four years, the broad flattened palms, that are such a feature of the fallow, begin to develop. Even when the antlers have reached full size there is an annual increase in the number of points or tines, and the general weight.

For much of the year, fallow deer live in separate sex herds which often overlap in range. By September the bucks have shed their antlers' outer covering of skin, known as the velvet. This prepares them for the rut when the females become ready to mate. During September and October, each male tries to establish a territory and assemble a group of females within it. It is a time of tremendous activity and noise, as bucks bellow to warn or challenge any intruder. They mark out their ground by pawing with their front feet and thrashing the head. Many nearby trees and bushes are also frayed, and sprayed with pungent urine.

The size and weight of a buck with a full spread of antlers is impressive, especially when seen from the position of a rival male. I managed to obtain such a viewpoint by fixing a cast-off pair of antlers firmly on to the front of a camera. The resident buck overlooked my otherwise human form and accepted the challenge. I mirrored his behaviour, so we walked side by side, and then our heads suddenly turned and the antlers met with a crash. This was early in the season and the males had not yet reached full vigour, so the attack was restrained. Within a week full combat between mature males resounded regularly across the parkland. For several minutes at a time a pair would engage antlers and press hard, moving first one way and then the other. Vegetation was gouged up on the tines, and the

Overleaf A barn owl at dusk.

antlers became draped in hanging grass as the beasts hurled themselves against each other. This time I viewed the scene from a safe distance, but I was close enough to see the sweat pouring from the combatants as one broke free and was chased from the stand. Breathing heavily the resident buck returned to his herd of females, having won the right to mate. Bucks do occasionally fight to the death. If a male, tired from seeing off one challenger, is attacked by another, he may be too weak to leave and it could be his last rut.

At Powderham confrontations are more frequent than in woodland or elsewhere in the wild, because the stands of individual males are much closer. Indeed, they resemble the leks of Scotland's fighting game, the black grouse cock. By the end of November the heat of the rutting season is at an end, and the deer once again graze quietly beneath the walls of the castle. Above, flights of duck wing in to overwinter on the mere and waterways crossing the estate.

The precious game, for which kings decreed punitive laws and landlords were willing to kill their countrymen, is now suffering the decline of many less illustrious creatures. Without large estates, our wildlife would be even poorer. If the countryside was managed in a way that allowed the return of the native grey partridge, other species would benefit too. Throughout the history of these islands, successive waves of wildlife and human cultures have spread across the land. Conquests and defeats, casualties and successes have all left their mark. Yet areas do remain where a rich and diverse wildlife survives remarkably intact.

During the first and last light of the day, when people are generally absent, the activity of wild animals is at its peak. In the twilight hours their acute sense of smell and hearing come into their own. After a day of filming, I made my way back on foot in the half light. A hare bounded to safety before sitting bolt upright, half facing away, to see what had caused the movement. A pheasant ran for cover while another called in the distance. The deer that were grazing alongside the wood melted silently back into the trees. Such is the secret nature of a country largely shaped by man. Animals such as these are the natural history of Britain – its past, its present and, hopefully, its future.

INDEX

Numbers in italics refer to illustrations.

Picture Credits

Pictures on the following pages were supplied by Bruce Coleman Ltd: 19 *top left* (Wayne Lankinen) & *top right* (Adrian Davies), 23 (John Fennell), 54 *left* & 55 *both right* (*all* Jane Burton), 62 *top* (Dr Eckart Pott) & *bottom left* (Peter Ward), 63 *top* (Jane Burton), 66 *left* (R. Wanscheidt), 66–7 *centre* (Jane Burton), 75 *bottom right* (Hans Reinhard), 87 *top left* (Bruce Coleman), 98–9 *all* (Jane Burton), 106 *left* (Roger Wilmshurst), 110 *top left* (Jane Burton) & *bottom* (Dennis Green), 119 *bottom* (Frank Greenaway), 138 *bottom* (Roger Wilmshurst), 150 (Jeff Dore), 158 *main picture* (Jane Burton) & *inset* (K. Weber), 159 *main picture* (Dr Eckart Pott) & *top inset* (Hans Reinhard), 162 *bottom left* (Dennis Green),182 (Werner Layer), 202–3 *left* & 203 *top right* (*both* Dennis Green), 203 *bottom right* (Gordon Langsbury), 206 *main picture* (Hans Reinhard) & *inset* (Gordon Langsbury) & 210 (Hans Reinhard).

Photographs on the following pages were taken by Roger Hosking, Wildlife Camera: 71 *top right*, 90–1 *right*, 123 *top*, 162 *top left*, 167 *top*, 190 *both*, 191 *bottom*, 194 & 214–15.

All other photographs were taken by Andrew Cooper.